Things I Learned from my Grandmother About Leadership and Life

(How to light a fire under People without burning them out)

(Second Edition)

Charles Ray

Uhuru Press

North Potomac, MD

The opinions contained in this book, except where they have been specifically attributed to an individual or institution, are the opinions of the author, and are not meant to represent the policy of the US Government or any institution, organization, department or agency thereof.

The reproduction or distribution, by any means, including electronic distribution, is expressly prohibited without the written consent of the copyright holder, except for fair use quotes in connection with reviews.

This book was originally published in 2008 by PublishAmerica, Baltimore, MD. ISBN: 1-60610-563-9

For information about this and other works of this author, contact the author at charlesray.author@gmail.com.

Printed in the United States of America

Cover design and interior illustrations by the author.

Copyright © 2018 Charles Ray

All rights reserved.

ISBN: 1986695360
ISBN-13: 978-1986695367

Dedication

I define leadership at the process that an individual uses to influence others to attain group or organizational goals. It is the process of changing the behavior and attitudes of others.

My objective as a leader is to achieve the organization's goals, or in military parlance, accomplish the mission, the minimum necessary expenditure of resources, and with minimum stress on those asked to do the heavy lifting. I don't say, you'll notice, zero stress, because a certain amount of stress is needed to move things, but without the unnecessary stress that leads to alienation and burnout. I want to motivate my followers to achieve more than they think they are capable of achieving, without destroying them in the process.

That was not always the case. There was a period in my life when I bought into the idea that the only route to success was driving myself and others. Work long hours, demand great sacrifice. Drive, drive, drive! Instead of success, what I achieved was an ulcerated stomach that nearly put an end to my career before it had even gotten off the ground. In fact, according to the doctor who treated me the second time my ulcers flared up and were on the verge of bleeding, it nearly ended my life.

Learning that something less than half the size of a number 2 pencil eraser was not only uncomfortable and painful, but potentially fatal was a wake-up call. I did a complete reassessment of my attitudes toward work and career. Achieving career goals was important, but so was the quality of life as I pursued those goals.

With the change in the demands I made on myself came a transformation of my views on how I should interact with my subordinates. If my work style had had such a devastating effect on me personally, what must it have been like for the poor unfortunates who had to follow me. I decided then and there that it was time to replace the stick with the carrot. For me, this led to a revolutionary discovery. I found out that you could actually get more out of people without resorting to coercive measures. If people were given clear goals, the resources to accomplish those goals, and a sense that they were more than mere cogs in some impersonal machine, they not only produced more, but they produced a better product. The key to getting things done, I learned, was not giving orders and driving people, but motivating them to commit to the organization's goals and to make those goals their own.

Even during my workaholic phase, achievement, not leadership was my goal. I have never sought power as an end in itself but have viewed it as a responsibility I must accept in order to achieve my goals. My goal is the destination, while leadership is the journey.

The idea for this book grew out of conversations I had with a young man named Michael Keller in 2004 and 2005. Michael was the economic reporting officer at the American embassy in Cambodia during the time I served as ambassador to that country. But, he was also my principal speech writer. We spoke often about my leadership style, which he described as easy-going but extremely effective, and in sharp contrast to the people he had previously worked for. We jokingly referred to my 'Techniques of Leadership for the Lazy.' There is, I reminded him, nothing intrinsically wrong with being lazy. If necessity is the mother of invention, then laziness is its father. After all, if mankind wasn't essentially lazy, we would still be content to carry bundles on our heads. One day, Michael suggested that I should write a book about my oddball philosophy of leadership.

My first reaction was, 'who needs another book on the subject?'. Besides, my way of doing things couldn't be all that unique. After all, I was not the first executive to suffer gastric distress. Surely, many other leaders have had the same epiphany. But, after a few years of observing government and private organizations in the US and abroad, I have come to the conclusion that I was overly optimistic. Stress and burnout continue to be major problems in many organizations, bullying in the workplace is a growing concern, and many organizations, especially in government, face a personnel crisis as baby boomers retire in increasing numbers—with insufficient replacements in the pipeline.

If the United States is to maintain its position in the world, economic, political, and military, something will have to be done. A critical area is a revitalized approach to leadership in all types of organizations. From my admittedly unscientific observations over several decades I have concluded that Americans, in particular those in leadership and management positions, take a perverse pride in working long hours, surviving on little sleep, and being deprived of quality time with their families. Ulcers, rather than being viewed as the unnecessary byproduct of wrongheaded ideas about work that can be fatal, are treated as the price of success.

As I rose higher in the government bureaucracy and found myself in charge of larger and more complex organizations, the discovery that this is the wrong approach to leadership has been of great value. As the organizations get bigger and the problems multiply no one person can deal with it alone—at least not for long, and never very effectively. Being able to set goals, provide guidance and resources, and get out of the way to allow your subordinates to 'do their thing' in job after job over the years since the late 1970 has been, for me, very successful. Despite creating cultures where work and fun go hand in hand; where family time is not a luxury, but a requirement; and where workaholism is actively discouraged, I created organizations that consistently excelled. In one instance I took over a poorly performing organization where 14-hour days were the norm. I instituted a routine 8-hour workday (no weekend work unless there was a crisis or emergency) and held happy hours and family days away from the work space. Within six months, not only had morale improved, but the organization was out=performing neighboring organizations by a wide margin based upon an inspector general report. We were not only producing *more* but were also doing a better job qualitatively. It had gone from a situation where people were trying to avoid being assigned to the organization to one in which we had, during the next assignment cycle, three and four people competing for each vacancy. Those already there in many cases asked to extend their tours of duty.

After thinking about it, I realized that Michael had been right. Not only was he an excellent speech writer, but he had seen something that had escaped my notice. There is a need to take a fresh look at leadership. Despite all the rhetoric about flat organizations, empowering people and the like, far too many people in leadership positions (and, notice here, I do not call them leaders, and the reason for that will become clear by the time you've finished this book) are still using techniques that put excessive stress on their organizations, and on themselves. Workaholics often make impressive gains in the short term. But, over the long haul they tend to fizzle. Worse, they often kill the spirit of those around them and leave organizations with problems that often don't surface until after they've moved on.

There are many excellent books on leadership available. Some of them are profound and some are funny. They all, however, chronicle the leadership traits and principles of famous people. In this book I've tried to describe leadership from the point of view of the average person, like you and me. While I do refer in some places to famous people (hey, I'm not that different from other writers), most of the examples I use here are from my own experiences and observations. I have included the failures as well as the successes because we can learn even from mistakes. In fact, if we are paying attention, it is from our mistakes and the mistakes of others that we learn the most.

One of the first problems I had as I began to write was how to distinguish between principles and practices so that the reader will clearly understand the differences. Principles are fundamental guides to why we do things, while practices are the 'what-we-do' in various situations. My philosophy is to adapt practice to a given situation based upon my fundamental beliefs, which over time are unchanging. I list those principles and then illustrated how they were put into practice either by me or by others. In a world of constant change, I believe it is important to have principle-centered leadership, because when core principles are internalized and shape our actions we are empowered to act in ways that are more appropriate to the situation. Leadership based on practice, or strictly by someone's 'book', stifles initiative and leads to actions that, while successful in some situations, don't necessarily work in others. Principle-centered leadership allows people at all levels of an organization to share responsibility and own the goals of the organization.

So, Michael, here it is—the book you suggested—the second edition. The lazy person's guide to leadership. This is how and why I do it. I hope it's what you had in mind.

And, last, but certainly not least, I dedicate this book to the memory of my grandmother, Sally Young (1889-1972), who, among the many things she taught me, taught me just about everything I know about leadership and dealing with people. She didn't have much formal education, but was the smartest person I've ever known, because she had something that's not very common these days—common sense.

Things I Learned From My Grandmother

About Leadership and Life

Charles Ray

Introduction to the Second Edition

My grandmother, Sally Young, was a tiny woman—a whisker under five feet in height and never weighed over 100 pounds in her life. She had very little formal education but taught herself to read well enough to be able to read the Bible from cover to cover, and her mathematical skills were basically only good enough to keep salesmen and merchants from cheating her. Despite the lack of education, or book learning, as she called it, she was one of the smartest people I've ever known.

Aunt Sally, as most people in our town called her, never owned a television, never went to a movie, and never flew in an airplane. The books she read were the Bible, an almanac, and the mail order catalogs that came regularly. She had an amazing memory, though, and could quote lengthy passages from the Bible, or remember obscure details from the almanac after only one reading. She also had sound judgment and a strong sense of right.

Charles Ray

Sally Young, 1889 - 1972

The daughter of a Native American man and an African-American woman who had been a slave, my grandmother grew up poor, with no opportunity to obtain formal schooling. In addition, as a double minority, there were few formal educational opportunities anyway. So, like many minorities at the turn of the century, what little education she got was at home and sporadic at best. She was taught to read the Bible and just enough arithmetic to be able to count her change at the market. Despite her small stature and lack of education she was a force in her community. When people had problems, they took them to Aunt Sally. When she spoke, people listened. When I was growing up, I took gramma, as I called her, for granted. She was just always there as grandmothers have been since the beginning of time. There with a hug when you needed it, a swat on the backside when you deserved it, and always with a witty little saying that to a youngster was just so much background noise. She knew the easiest way to do anything it seemed, from baiting a hook to flying a kite, and she always had a pithy little saying to go along with the skill. Some were sayings that everyone used, like 'don't cry over spilt milk.' Others, though, I think she just made up on the fly because they fit the message she was trying to get across, like, 'you can paint stripes on a skunk, but he's still no tiger, and he will still stink.'

It took me more than thirty years after her death to realize that I had, in fact, not only been listening to her, but I had internalized her pearls of wisdom. I had been leading government organizations for over thirty years at the time this book was first published, and by the time I retired from the U.S. Foreign Service in 2012, had logged over 50 years of government service (20 years in the army and 30-plus as a diplomat). That's half a century. I think I was moderately successful in most of those positions.

After deciding to write about the principles and

philosophy of leadership that have guided me, I spent a couple of years tossing it around in my mind. During that time, I encountered an obstacle—I couldn't decide to which school of leadership I belonged. Was I Type A or Type X? Did I manage by walking around or did I manage by exception? Did I lead from the front, from the rear, or from the middle of the pack? The fact is, at various times and under certain circumstances I have done or been all of these. The manuscript (and, I started it on an old Remington electric typewriter) went through several revisions over a two-year period, and each version ended up crumpled up in the waste basket. Why? Because it described HOW I did things, but I was failing to explain WHY. And, the reason I wasn't explaining why was because I was doing things reflexively rather than based upon some textbook or lecture, and I'd never sorted out in my mind why I was doing things. It's kind of like when you've been taught to hold the door for a lady or elderly person. You do it without really thinking about why.

Then, one day while I was riding the Washington Metrorail's Red Line on my way home from work, I noticed an elderly lady in my car gently chiding two teen girls who were playing their music too loud (illegal on the DC subway, but rarely enforced). They were disturbing the other passengers in their vicinity, but like most city dwellers, they just ducked their heads and frowned. Well, this little old lady got up, waggled her finger in their faces, and said something in a voice too low to be heard. But, boy, did it work. They bowed their heads in the universal gesture of shame and embarrassment and turned the volume way, way down. As I watched this, memories of my grandmother came flooding into my mind. I remembered how she and my mother used to hush us when we were being rowdy during church services with a withering glare, a voice so low you had to lean forward to hear it, and always, that waggling finger. She could, using a tone barely above a whisper, get us to snap to quicker than a bunch of recruits when a drill sergeant bellows at them.

And, in a flash, it came to me. My school of leadership, the philosophy that guided me for all those years of leading groups and organizations from military units to diplomatic establishments, to a diverse element of the Department of Defense, was just me doing it the way gramma taught me. It wasn't university training or military schools that had shaped the kind of leader I had become. That little voice inside my head, telling me, 'the only way to get finished is to get started,' was hers. The muse that inspires me to say, 'when the water gets deep, stop wading,' is my grandmother, still speaking to me as clearly as if she was standing at my elbow.

In the following pages, I have attempted to recall, collect, and explain as best I can what my grandmother taught me about leading and managing, and most importantly, about life. I include examples of other leaders that I think were successful, some famous, and some whose names you will not recognize. I can't help but think that each of them had a gramma, or an Aunt Sally who provided them with the solid foundation from which their leadership philosophy sprang. I hope you too will listen and learn as I did.

This is not a textbook or a scholarly work. I wrote things down as they came to me. And I try to explain them in simple, every-day terms. My goal is to explain how I managed to lead diverse groups of people in many different organizations over more than half a century. We live in a time of rapid and constant change and have to deal with the turmoil that change brings. It was that way for me, and with the accelerated pace of change presently, is no doubt even more so for leaders today. If we are to continue to be successful as a country, and if we are to weather the storms of change, we will need enlightened leaders to guide us. To those who helped me learn the ropes, even though I've forgotten most of your names, I thank you.

To my gramma, though, who laid the foundation, wherever you are, and I can just imagine you looking down on us, wagging that finger and shaking your head, thank you for all that you gave me.

A final note to readers. I've included a lot of new material in this second edition, covering events and experiences after the first edition was written, as well as illustrations to emphasize important points. If you like this book, please leave a review, even if only a few words, on the site from which you purchased it and on Goodreads.com. Reviews are how we independent authors get our books noticed by readers, so help an indie out. You have my thanks in advance.

Taking Charge - Begin at the Beginning

I began assuming leadership roles early in life. The funny thing about that, though, is that I never thought of what I was doing as taking charge, and never actively sought the mantle of leadership. Rather, I was just following my grandmother's injunction, 'do what needs to be done instead of waiting for someone else to do it.' The end result in most cases of my stepping up to get the job done was that the other people would just fall in and follow my lead and look to me for direction and guidance for future jobs. My informal leadership often became official leadership as I would be 'elected' head of the group or organization. That was how I became the youngest student council president in the history of our school; no one else wanted the jobs that the president had to do, I volunteered for the jobs, and ended up getting elected to the position. Now, at the time, I didn't think of what I was doing as leadership. I was just doing what needed to be done. The realization that I was exercising leadership came much later in life, after I'd left high school and joined the army. As my career trajectory took me to more senior and demanding positions, military and civilian, I began to see the significance of my earlier actions.

Now, this next bit of information is a shocker. Despite often finding myself in charge, until my late teens (around 14 or 15), I was a loner. Talking to other people was difficult, other than small groups of three or less—and, I had to know them well. If I was put into a situation where I had to speak to more than two or three people, my palms sweated and my mouth became as dry as a cotton boll on a summer afternoon. My situation was complicated by a national educational experiment that my school participated in, which involved the advance placement of students who scored high on specially designed examinations. My tests scores resulted in me skipping the final year of junior high school and beginning as a freshman the year I turned 13, a full year before I would normally have. Ours was a rural school, and a lot of the kids who lived on farms missed the occasional school year, so I ended up a freshman in class with kids two to four years older than me.

While I'd found my one year in junior high school difficult, with the increased social demands of the pre-teen years, that first year of high school was the most stressful and traumatic year of my life—and, don't forget, I did two tours in Vietnam during the war, and that year in high school made those two combat tours seem easy. I spent the first semester sitting quietly at the back of the classroom, hoping the older kids wouldn't notice the gawky kid who always turned in his homework on time, got straight A's in everything, and never spoke except to volunteer when the teacher wanted something done—provided it didn't involve talking in front of the class.

My home room teacher that freshman year, Ms. Paulyne Evans, was a perceptive person, though, and was dedicated to getting the most out of all of her students, whether they wanted to give it or not. She was also as stubborn as a Missouri mule.

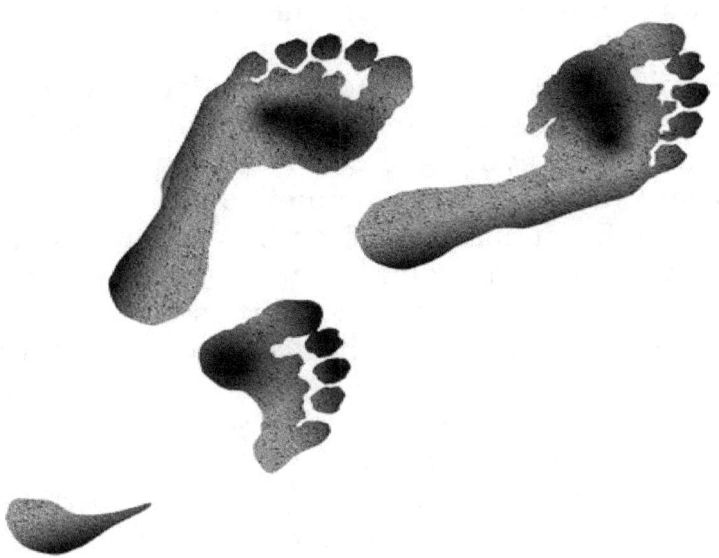

The only way to get finished is to get started.

She was my first encounter outside my immediate family with what is now known as 'tough love.' She recognized that I had the skills to get things done and that the only thing missing was self-confidence and comfort in dealing with groups of people. In order to bring me out of my shell, she gave me assignments that forced me to interact with others, not just my classmates, but the even older sophomores who shared the classroom with us (in our small, segregated school in Texas during the 50s and 60s, each teacher two grades, and all classrooms were shared by two classes from K through 12). By the end of the semester my fear of speaking in front of groups had eased a lot and was entirely gone by the middle of the next semester.

Despite being older, the other students accepted my leadership, primarily, I believe, because I was often the first one to do anything or come up with a solution to a problem. When student council elections were held after the Christmas/New Year break, without having put my name in nomination, I became the first freshman and the youngest person ever elected president, and I was reelected every year until I graduated in 1962.

During my four years in high school I learned how to influence people and events, set goals, and marshal the resources to accomplish those goals. I developed public speaking skills that served me well later as a professional. Most importantly, though, I learned that,

> **"The only way to get finished is to get started."**

Whenever we kids procrastinated or complained that we didn't know how to do something, my grandmother reminded us that the only to finish a job is to first get it started. This would seem obvious, but I have often been amazed over the years at the number of people who have difficulty just getting started on a task. In government, academia and in the private sector, we have thousands of people who just can't seem to get a project into the implementation stage.

I encountered this phenomenon during my first Foreign Service tour at the American Consulate General in Guangzhou, China in 1983. Younger readers will not remember a time before tablets and smart phones, or even desktop computers and word processors, but in the early 1980s, most government offices still produced documents on typewriters (electric fortunately) complete with carbon paper and rubber erasers—or, in some cases, little bottles of white paint, called WhiteOut™. The Department of State (referred to hereafter as the Department) was just introducing automation during this period. When I arrived in Guangzhou as a newly-minted Foreign Service Officer (FSO) in the spring of 1983. Documents were still being prepared in multiple copies on IBM Selectric™ typewriters, a most cumbersome way to do paperwork. Shortly after my arrival the Department shipped several boxes to the consulate general containing the components of the Wang Officer Information System (OIS)™, one of the early generations of automated word processors. Along with all the hardware was a box containing the manuals showing how to install and operate the system. What didn't arrive was a technician who could show us how to put the system together.

For several weeks the boxes sat unopened in our warehouse. In the consular section where I worked issuing immigrant visas to Chinese citizens, the question was often asked, 'when will we get the new system up and running', but no answer was forthcoming. Requests to Washington for assistance were met with silence, or the occasional unhelpful response, 'no help is currently available.' Like everyone else receiving the equipment, we in Guangzhou would have to deal with it in-house, meaning, we were on our own.' This generated groans and shrugs and everyone went back to their typewriters. The general mood seemed to be, if they really wanted us to do this, they would send some to help us, and since they're not doing that, it must not be important. To me this was an unacceptable situation. At the time, we were processing over a hundred immigrant visas per day, and the manual process we were forced to use caused some long work days. During a rare lull in the pace of work I asked my supervisor if I could take the manuals home to read. The answer was, yes, as long as it didn't interfere with my normal work, so I began the arduous process of becoming 'computer literate.'

When I felt comfortable with the new information I asked for permission to assemble the system. Since no one else had expressed any interest and the equipment was taking up much-needed warehouse space, my request was quickly granted. After a few false starts the system was up and running and I was given the unofficial title of consulate general 'systems manager,' and generally looked to as the in-house computer expert. Despite a lack of formal computer training, the label stuck and in two subsequent assignments (Shenyang, China and Chiang Mai, Thailand) I was assigned the responsibility for the information systems, which not only included installing new systems, but upgrading an existing network. I have no degree in computer science (my M.S. in Systems Management from the University of Southern California had to do with the holistic management of complex systems like hospitals, and included no computer-related courses in 1979 when I enrolled), and to this day I've only had one or two formal IT courses, I earned the respect of the few computer professionals we had at the time and since, and was frequently referred to during my diplomatic career as one of the few 'bosses' who knew how to use information systems effectively.

I learned two lessons from this experience. In addition to the wisdom of my grandmother's quip that the "only way to finish is to get started,' I learned that an 'expert' is someone who is willing to take a chance and do something that no one else understands, or cares to tackle.

I've given a lot of thought to this phenomenon. Why do so many people have problems with getting a project started?

I think fear of failure is probably a big reason. Our culture puts a high premium on success. Performance evaluations and compensation are often linked to success—or more accurately, to not making mistakes. Seldom have I seen a system that concretely rewards people for taking chances. I think far too many people have convinced themselves that if they don't start something that has the potential for failure, they will not fail, and as a result will be seen as successful. While that attitude might work for an individual in many circumstances, it does nothing to move an organization forward, and in the long run pulls the organization down. There is, on the other hand, another reason I believe explains the inability or unwillingness of some people to initiate new projects; not knowing what to do first. I ran into that problem when I began writing this book. I knew that I wanted to write about leadership and what it means to me, but I had a problem deciding how to start it. What do I say first? As I write these words, I can still hear my grandmother chuckle. If she'd been sitting near me as I stared at the blank sheet of paper in my typewriter, agonizing over that first sentence, she would have said:

> **"Start reading a book on page one."**

Okay, now you're saying, "Don't insult my intelligence. Everyone knows that." Think so? How many people do you know who can't help peeking at the last page of a mystery to see whodunit? What about the guy who tells you the ending of the movie you're about to see, or the score of the football game you missed, but recorded for later viewing? Unfortunately, there are a lot of people who skip page one when they start doing things, and try to go straight to the end, and in my experience, it never works out well. As to how that related to this book, my thinking went something like this; if you start reading on page one, that's where you should also start writing. Give the reader the logical beginning, and then go step by step from there. The same thing goes for any task. Start at the beginning.

There are a lot of people who don't take the time to understand the relationship between tasks, or steps in a task, and rush to the end without taking the necessary intermediate steps. Or, people who are intimidated by their vision of the end phase of a project, so they fear beginning. Like a deer caught in the headlights of an oncoming car, they stand and stare.

Things I Learned From My Grandmother

About Leadership and Life

Start reading a book on page one.

Getting things done in the proper order is important, even if you are not a ditherer. The opposite of the person who can never get started is the jack rabbit who skips the easy opening and jumps right to the middle—or even sometimes, the end. Whether you're a procrastinator or an impulsive, you put a strain on an organization because someone else usually has to pick up after you've gone, either by doing the job, or by doing it over.

The American Consulate General in Ho Chi Minh City (formerly Saigon), Vietnam is a textbook example of not starting at the right beginning point.

I had the honor of being selected to be the first American Consul General in the southern part of Vietnam after the U.S. established diplomatic relations with the country. Establishing an official American presence in a region of a Communist country that had once been independent, and a U.S. ally, was a daunting challenge and an historic event. As our relationship with a former enemy matured, it became important that our mission there accurately reflected the changes. It was all the more challenging because we were building the consulate general on the site of the former American embassy, and that dilapidated structure was to be demolished. The final product, I'm proud to say, is befitting a world power, and was admired by everyone who saw it. But, lack of adequate attention to the necessary first steps threatened it from the outset and made it a difficult project to successfully complete.

The architects who designed the building were anxious to create a structure that would be beautiful and unique, but they forgot that they were building a diplomatic establishment that had also had to be functional and in line with certain diplomatic protocols. After my arrival, which was at about the same time construction started, I held regular meetings with the project manager from State's Overseas Buildings Office (OBO), whose job it was to oversee the contractors working on the site. He brought updated site plans to each meeting, and often, he and I would don hard hats and walk the site. In one of our meetings, at a point when the second level of the building was being completed, we both noticed that an important, one might even say essential, component of any diplomatic establishment was missing. There was no flag pole on the design. To the architects this was probably an unimportant detail that had just been overlooked if they were aware of it at all. To anyone familiar with diplomacy, though, this was indeed a big thing. If you've ever visited an embassy or consulate, you no doubt take the presence of Old Glory for granted. It it's not flying proudly over the building, however, I guarantee you will notice.

There were a few anxious days as we scrambled to fix the problem. "If life gives you lemons, make lemonade." My grandmother didn't originate that saying, but if was one of her favorites. She never let problems stop her from getting what she wanted. If things were off track she found a way to take advantage of it.

The project manager and I put our heads together and tried to find a way to squeeze some juice from that particularly large lemon we'd been handed. We finally came up with the best pitcher of lemonade imaginable. We chose a spot in the front courtyard of the new building, an area that the architects intended for a little garden or something of that nature, and then we took the flag pole from in front of the old embassy building, and had it reconditioned. From the first-floor exterior walls of that building, which was in the process of being demolished, we took one of the granite blast shields and had a stonemason shape it into a terraced base for the pole. We then had a brass plate made, and inscribed with the history of the flag pole, and *voila*, we had not only solved the problem, but had made a little bit of history. Even local Vietnamese officials, some of whom had been our mortal enemies just a few decades earlier, were impressed by it.

I wish I could say that this was the only snag in that construction project, or that we caught all the others before construction was complete. When finished, it was indeed a beautiful building, but it had one particularly nasty problem which didn't make itself known until six months after we moved into the building and started operations.

The original design of the building included a beautiful interior garden between the public entrance and the entrance to the consular section. It was open to the sky and had decorative plants on each side and two fantastic murals on the stone walls. This provided a welcome counterpoint nuisance of security screening for our visitors, and a nice place to take a break from work. It quickly became one of the favorite places for visitors to pose for photos with the first U.S. Consul General (me), and thus, one of my favorite spots as well. So, what was the first step missed in this part of the project? Again, the designers focused on the final phase of the project and failed to do some basic research. Vietnam's weather is tropical, which means that for half the year you get daily monsoon rains. Open to the elements, the garden suffered a daily drenching during the first monsoon after we opened for business. The tile floors drained very well, but no outlet for all this water had been included in the plan, so the water flowed downhill into the nearest available area, the security screen area, where it shorted out the parcel scanning machine and X-ray gate on the first day.

Our normal diplomatic and consular work was disrupted for several days while we waited for technicians to come and repair the systems. We also brought in a local contractor to install a grated drainage channel in the space between the two areas. This was a disruption and added cost that could have been avoided if the designers had read carefully from page one of the project.

One final example of what can go wrong when you don't go through all the steps of a project before rushing to the finish was an incident I encountered during my tenure as ambassador to Zimbabwe, just before I retired from government service. At that time, the hardliners in Robert Mugabe's government took delight in giving me and my staff at the embassy a hard time. One of my staff was temporarily detained by guards at Mugabe's office for parking in an unmarked 'restricted' area. That little incident, while annoying, was not the real problem. He'd parked where he did to wait for an official visitor to one of our agencies who was staying in a rented house near that same restricted area. This was the first time the building was brought to my attention, and when I pointed out to the agency chief that in the event of a disruption in the government (such as the November 2017 coup that removed Mugabe from office) any visitors in that particular building could very well be cut off from the embassy, and we might have no way of helping them. That fact had not been considered when the building was rented several years earlier. Needless to say, I ordered immediate termination of the lease, and required that *all* future leases be reviewed by the embassy security officer before they were signed. Reading from the top of the page, and reading carefully—saves a lot of headaches, believe me.

Charles Ray

Never Forget, You are Leading People

I left East Texas in 1962 determined to see as much of the world as possible. Armed with a high school diploma from a segregated school, which, for an African-American in Texas during that time was about as useful as a three-dollar bill, I decided that the only way to accomplish my goal was to join the army. The service motto was 'Join the Navy and see the world," but up to that time the largest body of water I had ever seen up close was Lake Murval, a small body of inland water just north of the town I grew up in. I wanted to see the solid parts of the world, so I went for green instead of blue.

After basic and advanced training, I was sent to Germany, where I was assigned as a radio operator in the 24th Medical Battalion in Augsburg. As a lowly enlisted man my opportunities to exercise leadership were limited. I did volunteer one year to coach little league baseball, and I wound up with all the kids that the more experienced coaches had rejected, never won a game, and had a great time. Even though I didn't think of what I was doing as leading, I was, and I was learning. What I learned from that summer, combined with my grandmother's homespun wisdom set the stage for whatever success I have had since.

What I learned was that people are the most important component of any organization. And, by watching an expert 'people' person I learned the skills necessary to get the most out of that component.

My unwitting mentor during those early years was my battalion's first sergeant. Loren Walkup is the only leader from that era whose name I have never forgotten. A soft-spoken Native American who fought in the Korean War, he was a lot like my grandmother. During the two years I served under him I never heard him raise his voice. He was always there when you needed advice, and he had a way of expressing the most profound concepts or complicated subjects in language that was easy to understand. Looking back, I wonder how he ever got his paperwork done because he was always walking around the battalion area. From morning reveille to last call, 'Top' was a presence in the unit, from the motor pool to the mess hall; if you were there longer than an hour, you would see him. And, he didn't just walk. He interacted with the soldiers, and knew each of them by name, and knew a lot about them. Sometimes his interaction would be nothing more than chatting about the entertainment in the NCO club the night before, at other times he would be giving advice to a troubled GI, and at others he would be quietly correcting deficiencies he had noticed. Each of these conversations would be held in the same quiet voice.

His physical appearance was not that of the stereotypical warrior. He tended to be a bit on the cherubic (chubby) side. But, I think everyone of us in that battalion would have followed him to hell and back, and we worked hard to get things right, not because we feared punishment, but because we didn't want Top to be disappointed in us.

I recall an incident not long after I arrived in the unit, when I was asked (ordered) to move a vehicle from the motor pool to another area of the compound.

I had a driver's license issued to me by the unit based upon achieving an almost perfect score on the written test, but without a road test. My experience with motor vehicles up to that time had been limited to driving a cousin's old sedan from one edge of our property line to the other, a total of about one hundred yards. The military truck I'd been assigned to drive was way above my skill level, and I would up ramming it into a brick wall. The damage was minor, and I knew that I would be held responsible and my pay would be docked to pay for it. That, however, was not what worried me most. I was devastated at the thought that First Sergeant Walkup would be upset that one of his soldiers had screwed up.

Knowledge, technical skills, proficiency with the written and spoken word are all important for a leader, but I think that one of the most effective, essential, and important traits of a leader is that he or she be a people person. If you are not comfortable interacting with people of all kinds, work hard to overcome it— much as I was forced to do to overcome my fear of public speaking. Lacking the ability to communicate with and motivate others, in my opinion, you can never be more than a merely satisfactory leader. One of my grandmother's oddest saying was:

> **"Know every hen in the hen house."**

At first blush, this makes no sense, but I finally realized that she was referring to the need to know everyone you work with in order to more effectively lead them.

In 1861, Abraham Lincoln relieved General John C.

Fremont from command of Federal troops in Missouri. The general had made a lot of mistakes, including misuse of public funds, but for Lincoln, his biggest mistake was that he had lost the confidence of the men he led. He kept himself isolated from the troops and was out of touch with the situation in his area of responsibility. He had failed to walk around and it cost him his job. Had President Lincoln not been a leader who knew every hen in his hen house, it could have cost the nation considerably more.

Know every hen in the hen house.

When I was a kid, there was a farmer in our town who always bragged that he walked every inch of his fields every day and could tell you which corn stalk would produce the most ears of the sweetest corn. He claimed that he could walk into his barn and point out the cows that were the best milk producers and which were likely to have trouble calving at the end of the season. He used to say, "It ain't enough to grow it, you got to know it." He had half a dozen workers to take care of these seemingly mundane details but chose to do it himself. He didn't rely on second-hand reports, but his own direct knowledge. And, he had validation of his approach; the produce from his farm always commanded top prices at the market.

If you're the person in charge, it doesn't matter whether you are leading a platoon of 40 or an embassy of 600, it is essential that you be seen by and have contact with every person under your control on a regular basis. Here, I'm not talking about formal meetings, but the informal visits in your employees' work place, or about the area of your business. These casual contacts often have more meaning to the individual than formal sessions and conveys the message that you care about them as individuals. I have also found that this is an effective way to ferret out problems when they are still small and manageable, and amenable to easy solutions. People tend to be more relaxed and casual, and this level of candor allows them to bring up subjects that they would never dare talk about in a formal meeting. If you're to be a truly effective leader you should strive to create an environment that encourages your subordinates to be open and frank with you. When I welcome new people to my organization I tell them that I also welcome their ideas even if they disagree with my own. I maintain an actual 'open door' policy. The door to my office is always open unless I am involved in a private to classified meeting, and any member of my organization is welcome to come to see me with problems and ideas, or, if I'm not too busy, just to chat. Of course, more often than not, I visit them at their work stations where the same rules apply.

Public praise, private criticism. Few things are as demoralizing as working for someone who dresses you down or points out your mistakes in the presence of others. When you engage in this type of activity, not only do you alienate the target of the criticism, but it has a negative impact on those who witness it as well.

> **"Kiss 'em on the front porch, but spank 'em in the woodshed."**

When I was deputy chief of mission (DCM) of our embassy in Sierra Leone, a country on the coast of West Africa, I had an office that overlooked the street in front of the embassy. I was only a few floors above the street, and when the window was open, which it often was to take advantage of the ocean breeze, the sounds from outside were clearly audible. One morning I heard a commotion and when I looked out my window I saw one of our American employees dressing down one of the Sierra Leonean staff on the sidewalk, It was a busy day, and hundreds of visa applicants were lining the sidewalk up to the building's entrance. From my vantage point I could see that not only was this an extremely embarrassing situation for the unfortunate employee, but it was attracting the attention of the people waiting in line to enter the embassy, and other employees in the vicinity as well. A situation was developing that went beyond mere internal morale. This had the potential to affect the opinion that Sierra Leoneans had about the United States. One silly argument could set back our efforts to build goodwill among the populace.

Kiss 'em on the front porch, but spank 'em in the woodshed.

My first instinct was to rush down and put a stop to it, but my grandmother's 'woodshed' saying saved me from making a bad situation worse. If I had gone down and remonstrated with the American employee in front of everyone, I would be just as guilty as he was. So, I calmed down and then sent my secretary (now known as office management specialist, or OMS) down with instructions to quietly ask the American employee to come to my office immediately. When he arrived I calmly explained why his behavior was inappropriate and the possible fallout from it. He was an otherwise valuable employee and I didn't want to alienate him—just correct his behavior. Seeing that I didn't appear to be angry, nor was I using a harsh tone with him, he acknowledged the problem and apologized for his behavior. I suggested that he go back down and apologize to the Sierra Leonean employee in public, and then, if there was a problem, take him some place private and talk to him about it. A few days later he came to my office and thanked me for the advice. He said his encounter had been the result of a misunderstanding and by dealing with it in private the matter had been quickly and effectively settled. As an added bonus, the local employee was so impressed by his public apology they had become friends.

This principle is so important, I will repeat it. 'Praise in public, criticize in private.

> **"Two horses can pull a heavier load than one horse can."**

Have you ever tried to move a piano by yourself? Kind of hard to do, isn't it? Getting most jobs done in an organization is much the same. Trying to do it all yourself is a recipe for disaster, or at best a job not done as well as it could be. While it might be true that some tasks are better done by one person acting alone (painting a masterpiece, for instance), the overall health of an organization depends upon the members acting together, and that includes the person in charge.

Effective leaders are networkers, building strong personal and professional alliances constantly. The most effective are those who build what I think of as 'global' alliances. Global alliances are ties and connections in all directions—up, down, and sideways. For me, upward alliances are with those who can serve as mentors and facilitators. These relationships do not necessarily have to be with people in your organization or chain of command, although it is important to maintain those as well. A relationship that served me exceptionally well for two decades was with a person who was only once in my formal chain of command. The late Mary Ryan, who served as the State Department's Assistant Secretary of State for Consular Affairs, was a friend, confidante, and advisor to me from 1988 until her death in 2005. In fact, the only time she was not knowingly my mentor was from 1983 to 1987 when I served in consular positions and was ostensibly a part of her command responsibility. It was during this time, she once told me, that I came to her attention, when I had to handle a particularly sensitive consular case involving an American citizen who had accidentally started a hotel fire by smoking in bed, which caused the deaths of several people. I was on my second tour of duty, had not yet been tenured, and, because of the distances involved, and the sorry state of communications, I was forced to handle the case often without any kind of guidance from my supervisory chain of command. It wasn't lost on her that it was finally resolved favorably, based in large part on the unilateral actions I took in the field. It was in 1988, however, when I served in Thailand and only occasionally had to perform consular service as a back-up for our one consular officer in Chiang Mai that I directly sought her advice on a case involving the murder of an American citizen. From that point on, she was always available for advice and assistance, and we corresponded regularly on matters large and small.

Despite the disparity in our ranks, I was a relatively junior officer and she was already at the top rank of the Foreign Service (career ambassador), we developed a friendship that endured until her death.

During the early years she gave me career advice that helped me advance through the ranks. As I achieved higher levels of responsibility she became my sounding board and reality check. She was more, though, than just an advisor. She directly helped me advance in my career. In 1987, I was selected to be the first American consul general in Ho Chi Minh City, Vietnam. This was a historic moment. The United States had only recently established diplomatic relations with our former enemy and having an American presence in the south where the bulk of our economic and consular activities were centered was in the spotlight. The position was graded at the Senior Foreign Service level, and a number of highly-qualified senior officers were interested in serving. At the time, I was a student at the National War College in Washington, DC, and while I had officially requested consideration for promotion into the Senior Foreign Service, I had not been promoted. I had also expressed interest in serving in Vietnam, naming the consul general position as my first choice. I had the support of ambassador-designate Douglas 'Pete' Peterson and Vietnam country director, Marie Huhtala, but the personnel system was reluctant to pick me over the more senior candidates. It was only long after my eventual selection that I learned that Mary, as a voting member of the committee that was responsible for making the final recommendation to Secretary of State Madeleine Albright, had insisted that I be the candidate recommended. A year into the job I was promoted into the Senior Foreign Service at the rank of counselor, so my rank finally matched the job. Throughout the 40 months that I held the job, Mary was always available, by email or face-to-face on my occasional visits to Washington, for advice and counsel as I learned on the job. Thanks to her, I was able to play a small part in U.S. diplomatic history, and any success I had in the job is largely due to her.

Establishing upward alliances is important, but even more important in most cases are those relationships you forge with people who are below you in the hierarchy. You can't be a leader without followers.

Like the captain of a ship, as a leader your job is to determine the destination of the vessel and communicate this to the crew. It's up to the helmsman and the engine room to get the ship to its destination. You must clearly communicate what you want, make sure you have provided the necessary training and resources, and trust that they will follow your instructions faithfully. They, in turn, must trust that you have done your job well, that your instructions are correct, and the tools that have been provided are appropriate and adequate.

Building this trust in your subordinates requires a lot of time and effort, but the payoff is worth the investment. Whatever the other demands of your position, carve out time for the people at all levels.

Charles Ray

Two horses can pull a heavier load than one horse can.

This time should be face-to-face, giving you the opportunity to get to know their strengths, weaknesses, and desires. Let them know that you think of them not merely as names on an organization chart, but unique individuals who have something of value to contribute to the organization's mission. Encourage them to learn and grow, and to challenge themselves. While you're getting to know them, let them know you. Seeing you in person is far better that the best written formal memos and letters, or the most stirring speeches, because it is through direct contact that you convey your commitment, and in most cases, this will be reciprocated by their commitment to you and the organization. You need to let your people see that you are just what you appear to be, that your commitment to them and the organization is real. In most military and civilian government organizations there are formal methods to compel obedience and compliance to directives, but coercion is limited in its effectiveness, and can enforce action only in specific instances. It cannot compel commitment.

In 1999, Secretary of State Albright decided to pay a visit to the newly-opened consulate general in Ho Chi Minh City. We went into overdrive preparing for this historic visit, preparing briefings, tours, and meetings. As consul general, my role was to determine the overall theme of the program, assign duties, and ensure that everyone understood their tasks and carried them out, on time and according to plan.

As was my usual practice, I spent time each day with each section chief, as well as various individuals, rehearsing their roles to make sure everything would go smoothly. Included in my daily rounds were chats with the consulate custodial staff. These were brief, entirely casual encounters, little more than asking them about their health and their kids, and sometimes having a cup of sweet iced Vietnamese coffee with them on their rest breaks.

My front office staff (primarily my deputy and my office management specialist) thought this was a waste of valuable time that could have been better spent elsewhere, but since I was the 'boss' and had been doing this from my first day on the job, they just shrugged, after one mention of it, and I'm sure when I wasn't around, they chuckled at the 'old man's' eccentricities.

On the day of Albright's visit, I arrived early to check last-minute preparations. My deputy came into my office, shaking his head and with a bewildered look on his face. When I asked him what was up, he said that he'd come in at 5:00 am, just a few minutes before me, to do his own checks, and had found the custodians polishing the marble entrance way to the building. This had not been on our list of tasks, and no one had directed them to do this. When he asked them why they were doing it, one of them said that they wanted to ensure the steps were spotless when the secretary arrived, so she would think well of 'their' building. One of them would remain at the entrance to wipe away any smudges or stains right up until the moment of her arrival. Now, that is commitment. It can't be commanded, only earned.

It's lonely at the top, but it is not necessary to be alone. With all the upward and downward alliances, as a leader, you ultimately bear the sole responsibility for the success or failure of your organization. This load can be lightened if you have an effective network of peer relationships—those lateral connections.

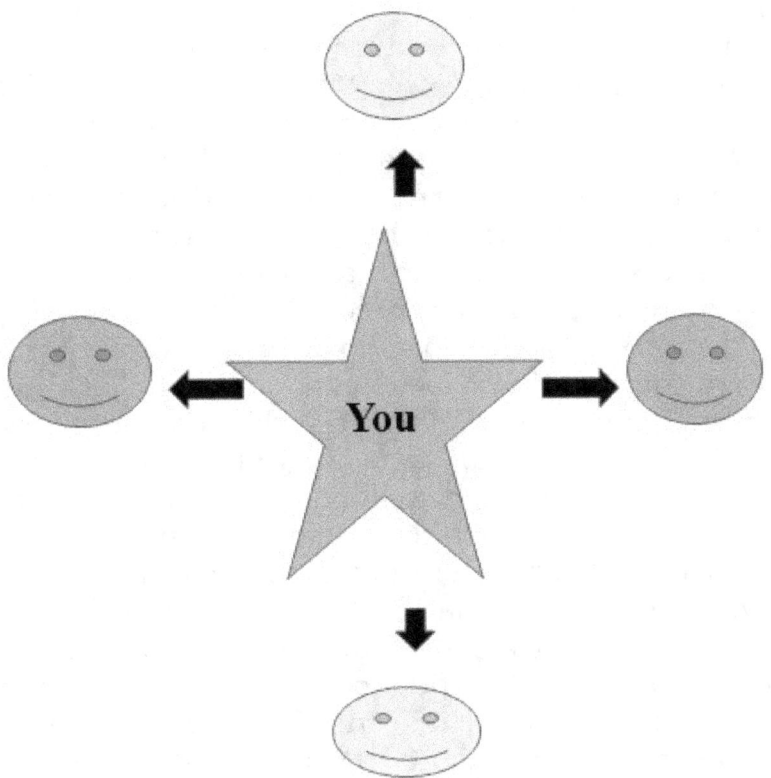

Multi-directional relationships and networks are important

We all have issues on occasion that are not appropriate to discuss with either superiors or subordinates. Having a colleague you can trust and with whom you can be candid is a great stress reliever. This kind of relationship can't be forced or developed quickly. It evolves over time, usually growing out of shared interests and experiences. I have one friendship that has endured for more than half a century. Upon seeing the two of us together for the first time you wouldn't imagine that we could ever become friends. He was a husky, athletic type with a girlfriend in every town in Shelby County where we grew up. I, on the other hand, was the skinny, awkward bookworm who had trouble talking to girls, and more often than not could be found in a corner with my head buried in a book. But, William King and I were the only boys in our high school class, and we were neighbors who shared a love of the outdoors. For four years, it was the two of against the world. After graduating from high school, we went our separate ways, but we kept in touch, and when we met every five years of so, we just picked up where we left off. Bill is someone I know that I can tell anything and rely on a sympathetic hearing. Even more important, if I tell him something in confidence, he keeps it just between the two of us. Every leader needs a Bill in his life.

Another relationship that is part peer, part subordinate, is a leader's interaction with his or her number two. The second highest ranking person in the hierarchy occupies a tricky position, one with a lot of responsibility, but with limited authority. The title might be deputy or executive officer, but the person who is there, who is responsible for taking over in your absence, is different from the rest of the people in the organization. This person is your alter ego and should be privy to most of your inner self if the organization is to continue functioning smoothly during those times when you have to be away. A sense of absolute trust is this person—in fact, a sense of absolute two-way trust—is the most important trait to look for when selecting a deputy. If you inherit a deputy from a predecessor, make it a priority to develop that trust. In both of my assignments as an ambassador, I inherited the deputy chief of mission from the previous ambassador and had them on the job for a year as they finished their tours of duty. The efforts I put into building trust were worth it. Both organizations were in turmoil, though not related to my arrival, and this sense of trust that enabled us to work effortlessly together was absolutely essential.

Charles Ray

What It Takes to Be a Successful Leader

Deciding which traits are essential for success as a leader is a lot like arguing about how many angels can dance on the head of a pin. As my grandmother would say, 'it depends on who's counting, and how big the pin is.' Everyone has a different list. Are there three, seven, twelve, or twenty essential traits? Until I started writing this chapter, I had honestly never thought seriously about it. After several months of making lists, tearing them up, and starting over, I have settled on the following traits as absolutely necessary if you wish to be successful as a leader—at least, I have found that to be the case for me personally, and have observed them in others I think of as great leaders. Not, mind you, that I think of myself as a *great* leader, but I do believe I turned in a good performance during my fifty years of service.

Character and Integrity

In order to be successful in accomplishing its mission an organization must have a system of shared values among its members. The glue that holds these values together is the sense of honesty and integrity transmitted by the leadership and owned by the membership. My grandmother was basically a gentle woman who seldom lost her temper, but she would erupt in anger whenever she detected that someone was lying to her. Woe be unto the errant grandchild caught fibbing—this was a guaranteed trip to the woodshed, and worse, she would make you take the long walk to the front yard where you would have to select your own switch from the big hedge that fronted the yard, and heaven help you if that switch did not meet her exacting standards. But, she firmly believed that a person's good name was the most important of his or her possessions. As kids, we could often talk our way out of punishment for most of the annoying little things we did—but, never dishonesty.

> **"Your reputation is what you show to others in the light, but your character is what you show yourself in the dark of night."**

You can't describe your character or integrity, you must demonstrate it. If your followers are to accept it, it must be sincere. It must be evident in every word and action. People want to be part of something meaningful. A strong sense of shared values in an organization serves to motivate people to achieve beyond their expectations. When every member of an organization feels ownership of the goals and values of the organization, great things are possible. How, though, does a leader get the members of an organization to commit to a shared value system? The answer is simple; by example. It is the responsibility of the leadership of an organization to instill organizational values and ethics by constantly living up to the standards that underpin those values. Every word and every action of a leader should be shaped by the stated values of the organization. Even in small ways values and ethics are transmitted.

In most government offices, especially our embassies and consulates abroad, we deal with sensitive and classified documents on a daily basis. Each of our embassies has a U.S. Marine Corps security detachment that has the duty to check all offices each day to ensure that all such documents have been properly secured. When they find sensitive or classified material that has been left unsecured, they lock it in their office and leave a notice of 'Security Violation or Infraction' on the desk of the offending party. Too many of these violations can have a negative impact on a person's career. Infractions can earn letters of reprimand, and if the violations continue, can also short circuit promotions or assignments.

When I was DCM at our embassy in Sierra Leone, in addition to our regular diplomatic duties we had to contend with a violent civil war that was tearing the country apart. All the competing demands and the fast pace of events, along with the sheer volume of classified and sensitive information we had to handle, put a great deal of stress on everyone in the embassy.

An incident that took place rather early in my tour of duty illustrates, I believe, just what I mean about the importance of integrity, especially in a leader.

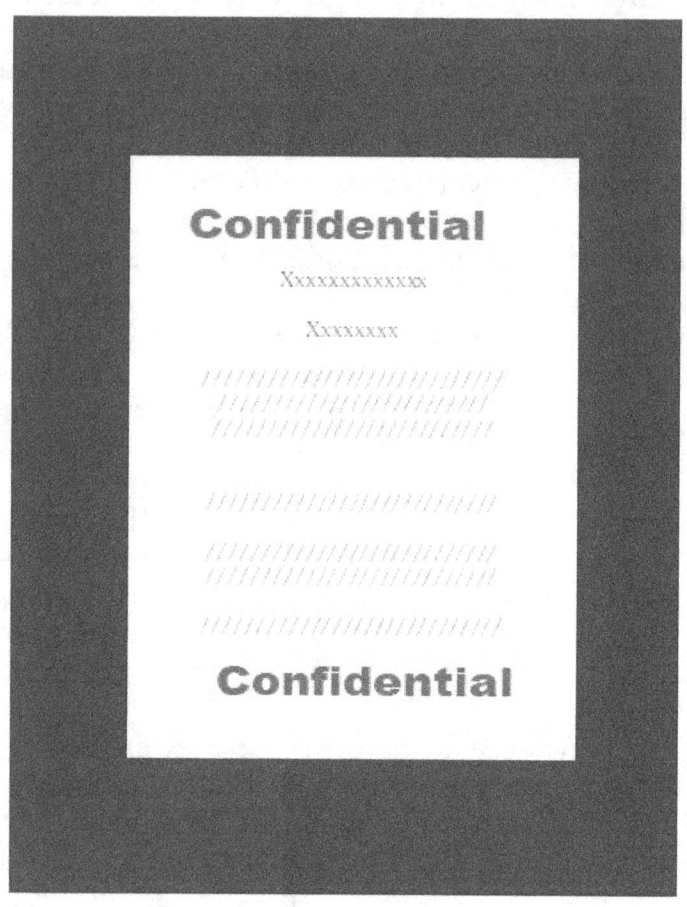

Late one afternoon, I was working on a particularly sensitive document when I received an urgent summons to the Foreign Ministry. My secretary (the title hadn't been changed to OMS at this time) was not at her desk, but I assumed that she had only stepped out for a moment, so I put the document into her in-tray, secured my own office, and rushed off to my appointment. The meeting ran late, so when it ended, I went home.

The next morning when I arrived at the embassy I found my secretary nearly in tears. She had arrived early to prepare for the day and found a 'Notice of Security Infraction' on her desk. She assured me that she had properly secured her desk and work space before leaving for the day and had no idea how a classified document came to be left in her in-tray. It didn't take me long to realize that her 'infraction' was from the document that I'd put there. Since our offices were considered 'secure' spaces, the infraction was considered minor, but it left her visibly upset nonetheless. There was nothing on the document itself that identified any particular individual and it would have been easy to simply ignore it. After all, it was her first infraction, and wouldn't impact her career. No one knew I'd put the document there, and with my known record of sensitivity to such matters, no would have ever thought it was me. But, I knew. I also knew that my grandmother would have been ashamed of me for not owning up to my mistake.

I explained to my secretary what had happened, and then went to the Marine Security Guard office and had them cancel her infraction and issue it to me instead. It demonstrated far better than any document or fancy speech could what I stood for. Honesty and integrity are not just buzz words, but are an integral part of what I am. I could not earn the trust and respect of the people in my organization by making speeches. That was earned by acting on the principles that I espoused.

People want leaders they can trust to do the right thing and be truthful even when the news is bad. Always standing for honesty and integrity will gain greater respect and support, I firmly believe, than any other character trait.

Communication Skills

The greatest idea is worthless if it cannot be communicated effectively to those who must carry it out.

In 1964, I was selected to attend the army's Officer Candidate School (OCS) at Fort Sill, Oklahoma in preparation for commissioning as a second lieutenant in the artillery. I have only a vague recollection of the chaotic events of those eight or nine months. There was lots of yelling, pushups, running everywhere, and vain efforts to comply with impossible orders barked at us by more senior officer candidates. There is one incident, though, that stands out clear in my memory after all these years, and it illustrates the importance of effective communication.

It was a balmy September evening when I stepped off the bus that carried a group of us from Oklahoma City to the OCS reception center at Fort Sill, just outside the town of Lawton. It had been an uneventful ride, none of us had a clue what awaited us, and I had just come all the way from Augsburg, Germany, and was too tired to even care. Middle class candidates with their bright green shoulder tabs, acted as unit sergeants, and they performed their roles with relish. Instructions weren't spoken, they were screamed, and often countermanded in the same breath. To say that I was immediately confused and disoriented is a gross understatement. For a few moments I seriously considered getting back on that bus and trying to make my way back to Germany. These guys, and back in those days they were all male, had never learned how to be real noncommissioned officers from the liked of First Sergeant Loren Walkup. They acted like caricatures of tough drill sergeants from a really bad B movie. Trust me, even in those days before the army put a stop to hazing, drill sergeants in basic training didn't yell that much.

Anyway, after several minutes of chaos—that seemed like hours—we were formed into groups and jogged to the buildings that would be our home for the duration of the course. Once inside the building, we were assigned bunks and told to get our gear ready for inspection. At this point, a senior candidate put in an appearance. I don't recall his name or what he looked like, just those coveted red tabs he wore on his shoulder, signifying that he was only weeks away from graduating and commissioning, and the wicked looking 'swagger stick' he used to emphasize his words. A small digression to explain something to readers who are unfamiliar with archaic military jargon. A swagger stick is a short, metal-tipped baton that in the old army was traditionally carried by officers. I understand that they have since been outlawed, and frankly I am one who does not mourn their passing. His was only about twenty-four inches long, jet black with a silver tip, but when he waved and poked it at you it looked as long as a spear. Each one of us new guys got poked that night, but, for reasons that to this day are unclear, I seemed to be the focus of his attention.

He came over to where I was sitting on the edge of my bunk trying to get my socks into a military fold and used me as his 'training aid' for the rest of the room.

When he wanted to show them the proper way to wear the insignia that identified us as new candidates, I got poked on the collar bone. Stressing that we were no longer enlisted and would therefore no long be authorized to wear our rank on our sleeves, he gave me a light tap on the biceps. It didn't hurt but it was a nuisance and a distraction. I honestly can't remember much of what he said because my attention was focused on that damned stick.

What I do remember is that he seemed obsessed with how he wanted our combat boots to look. It was important, for instance, that they always be mirror-shiny, and I got poked on the toe when he told us how to shine them. Then, he said he wanted each of us to put a red dot on the instep of our left boot, topping the top of my foot as he spoke. What I heard was 'red dot on instep of left boot,' but all I saw was that stick poking my instep.

Now, here's the problem with his communication technique. He was allowing body language (gesturing with the stick) to override verbal communication, and he didn't know beans about the human foot. You see, he was tapping the correct part of my foot, but what he really meant to say was that he wanted the red dot on the arch, or bottom of the boot.

The next morning when he came to inspect us before morning I was the hit of the barracks. Both pairs of my boots were shining like glass, and the pair I wasn't wearing were lined up under my bunk with razor-like precision. Furthermore, on the instep of each of my left boots was a precisely-drawn red circle done with fingernail polish that one of my enterprising bunkmates who'd been told in advance to be prepared had brought with him. Those circles were artistic masterpieces, and they were drawn right on the spot that he kept poking.

I missed breakfast that morning, spending what time I had before the first class removing the offending spots and re-drawing them on the bottom, which is where he wanted them.

I learned a valuable lesson from that humiliating experience. One; as a communicator, make sure you're saying what you mean to say, and don't *do* anything to detract from your message, and two; if you're the recipient of a confusing message, ask for clarification. I can only hope that my upper-class colleague learned from that experience as well.

> "What you do speaks louder than what you say."

In the previous section I wrote about the importance of honesty and integrity. Without these, leadership is merely management, and ineffective management at that. Without effective communication it is wasted effort. Ethics shapes the culture of an organization, but it takes communication to convey those ethical standards, and the procedures that make a leader's vision reality.

Communication is used inside the organization to motivate employees to 'own' the goals and missions, and outside the organization to explain it to others. Whether you're making widgets for the commercial market, educating students, or carrying out government policy, communication is the tool you use to make it happen.

Every summer since 2014, I've run a workshop on professional writing for Rangel Foreign Affairs Program scholars at Howard University in Washington, DC. I tell my students in the first session that, whether a communication is written, verbal, or nonverbal, there are only three reasons to communicate, and it's as easy as pie to understand:

Persuade
Inform
Entertain

To **Persuade** is to get someone to do or not do something. In the State Department, when you want someone to take an action, you prepare an action memorandum, which lays out the desired course of action, complete with justification. If you write to your sweetheart, or speak to him or her on bended knee, to propose marriage, you are communicating to persuade.

When you're not looking for a particular action, but you wish someone to have specific knowledge of a subject, you write to **Inform**. Again, using the State Department as an example, information memoranda are used to prepare officials for trips, for example, by providing advance knowledge of places being visited, the personalities they will meet, and the main subjects that will be discussed. An action memo will probably have been used to convince the official to take the trip.

Finally, if you wish merely to amuse or **Entertain**, you can write a story, tell a joke, or perform a juggling act.

Each of these objectives will also *influence* the target audience, but when you write to inform, this is also another way of saying to influence, as you are shaping the universe of the audience's knowledge.

When I give this lecture, I challenge my students to come up with another reason to communicate, and to date haven't had a taker.

So, if your communication is to be effective, you

must have firmly in mind your objective. Knowing that is the starting point of all communication. Before you open your mouth, pick up a pen, or reach for the keyboard, ask yourself the following questions:

1. What is the purpose of this communication?
2. Who is my audience?

The answers to these two questions will help shape how you convey your message and should be kept in mind through the process. If your intent is to instruct employees on a new process that has many complicated steps, clear written instructions, supported by face-to-face meetings is probably called for. If, on the other hand, you are trying to gain support for a new policy initiative, talking it over with the principal stakeholders before putting the first word on paper is usually more effective. Gaining commitment to shared corporate values is achieved primarily through nonverbal communication. Employees who see you living the principles of ethics and honesty get the message far better than they will from reading memos about it. If you write it or just say it, they know you said it. If you 'walk the talk' they know you mean it.

Leaders must be effective public speakers. The leader is usually the public face of the organization and is usually the symbol by which the organization is judged. If you are not at ease speaking before an audience, take steps to overcome it, or find your 'Paulyne Evans' to help you get over it.

> **"You have to get in the water if you want to learn how to swim."**

Public speaking is like any other skill, despite the fact that more people probably fear speaking to an audience than fear death. You should seek opportunities to speak to audiences, starting small if you're uncomfortable, and sticking to subjects that you know extremely well. Like swimming, as you gain skill, you can venture into deeper water. No matter how comfortable you get, though, never lose sight of the basic principles. What is the purpose of this speech and who am I talking to?

An excellent way to develop your skills before an audience is to join a chapter of your local Toastmasters Club. This will help you learn the techniques of public speaking and since you will be speaking to an audience that has the same goal as you do, conquering the fear of speaking in public, the stress should be far less.

Along with the standard speaking techniques I have found that story-telling and humor can be excellent ways make audiences more responsive to your message. When I am talking to my subordinates I often buttress my arguments with a story or an adage, sometimes made up on the spot to fit the message I'm trying to convey. A pithy adage like 'you can paint stripes on a house cat but it still won't be a tiger' will be remembered, and hopefully the point you are trying to make will as well. Humor, effectively used, is also an excellent way to break through to an audience that might not welcome your message, or you.

When I was serving as State's Diplomat-in-residence at the University of Houston (TX) during the 2005-2006 school year, I was assigned to substitute for the secretary of state at a dinner to raise scholarship money for minority students, because she was unable to come to Texas to participate. It was obvious when I entered the ballroom that the people who had shelled out big bucks for the dinner were disappointed that at not getting to hear the secretary speak, and more than one curious—and not too friendly—glance was thrown at this unknown person mounting the stage with the master of ceremony, a well-known local TV news anchor. The emcee sensed the tension in the room, and in an effort to put the best face on things read my entire biography as an introduction. As you might imagine, with over 40 years of total government service at that point in my career (including 20 years in the military), there's no way it can be given in detail in a short introduction. So, she went on until she'd pretty much covered it all, outlining my career from my enlistment in the army, from a small town just 190 miles north of Houston, through my many diplomatic assignments—I had just finished a tour as ambassador to Cambodia. As she spoke, I noted a lot of people paying more attention to their water glasses than to her, as if to say, so what, he's still not the secretary of state.

This was clearly going to be a tough audience, and if my speech bombed, it would reflect poorly, not only on me, but on the reputation of the Department of State as well. When I finally stood at the dais, I paused and scanned the audience. This unaccustomed silence caused almost every eye in the room to focus on me. I then pushed my prepared speech aside and said, "I know you are all wondering who this person standing here before you is; and I confess that after hearing that introduction, I'm wondering myself. Such praise is usually reserved for a eulogy, so I never expected to hear it. I do know that I signals that I must really be getting old, when my introduction is longer than my speech."

The room exploded in laughter, and when they finally quieted down, I went back to my prepared speech, which I peppered with a few one-liners; sensing that this audience liked a little humor with their after-dinner speeches. After the speech, as I circulated through the room shaking hands and greeting people, several remarked that it was the best dinner speech they had ever attended and they were glad I came. My grandmother wouldn't have been surprised at the outcome. As she would've said, 'get 'em to laugh, and you got 'em.' Now, I did what I did out of desperation, but it worked. I have used it several times since—never with the same audience—and it still gets laughs.

Another technique that I mention above, that is also very effective—the pause before speaking. Whenever I stand in front of an audience, I spend several seconds making eye contact with as many people as possible before speaking. Silence is a great attention getter. If you want to get your message across you have to get the audience's attention.

Things I Learned From My Grandmother
About Leadership and Life

**Get 'em to laugh, and
you got 'em.**

Which reminds me of a story I heard as a child about the Missouri mule.

A farmer in Missouri had a stubborn old mule that just would not plow a straight line or follow any other instructions no matter how loud the farmer yelled. One day, as he was vainly trying to get the mule to plow, a stranger was walking by. Seeing the old farmer's problem, the stranger approached the fence.

"Mister," he said in a lazy drawl. "For five dollars I'll get that old mule to plow as straight as a ruler."

The farmer was at the end of his patience and was seriously considering sending the mule to the glue factory, so he agreed.

"Go ahead, stranger," he said. "If you can make this old sack of useless bones do anything, it'll be worth five dollars."

The stranger climbed over the fence and started making his way across the poorly plowed field. On the way, he stopped and picked up a piece of board that had been left over from when the fence was put up. When he reached the two, he stopped directly in front of the old mule. Man and mule eyed each other warily. Then the stranger swung the board and whopped the mule right between the eyes.

Startled, the farmer shouted, "Whoa, stranger, I thought you said you were going to teach my mule to plow straight, not whack him on the noggin."

Smiling crookedly at the farmer, the young man replied, "Oh, I'm gonna teach him all right, but first, I had to get his attention."

Writing is the other traditional form of communication that is important to effective leadership. The same basic questions apply and the techniques are similar, although I rarely try to be funny in writing except when I'm penning one of my works of fiction, unless in an official document it's my goal to entertain along with whatever other objective(s) I might have. I find, though, that attempts at written humor tend not to have the same impact as spoken jokes and can often backfire. I believe this is because of the lack of body language that can help provide the nuance of meaning that helps an audience 'get' the joke. Unless you're writing to someone you know very well, it's best to keep your sense of humor in check. Of course, as you can see from my use of the story about the Missouri mule, I often don't follow my own advice.

Of the three forms of communication, written, spoken, and nonverbal, I think that nonverbal is the most important, and the most difficult to control. The problem with nonverbal communication is that you are sending messages, often without being aware that you're doing so. The only advice I can offer for that is to develop awareness. Watch how people respond to you, particularly if their reactions are not in line with what you're saying. It could be that what you're *doing* in terms of body posture, facial expression, or gestures, is louder than your words. Put yourself in the place of your audience and ask yourself, "What does that action mean?' Remember that communication is a two-way process, and nonverbal communications are always taking place whether you intend it or not and, if you're not careful, can be contradictory. Take, for example, the boss who announces an open-door policy, but then keeps his office door closed or who is rarely seen outside the office. A friend once told me of a boss he had who did just that. He issued an open-door memo, but kept his office door closed, and arranged it so that a large plant blocked the view of his desk from the door. Further, he required that anyone wanting to see him had to make an appointment with his secretary. Needless to say, regardless of the sincerity of his memo about having an 'open door,' his actions spoke far louder.

The Ability to Deal with Change and Uncertainty

In business and in government—in fact, in life—change is constant, and the only certainty is uncertainty. As my grandmother would say:

> "The sun don't shine on the same dog's back every day."

If that sounds strange, that's only because it's a country woman's way of saying that things are always changing. It's similar to a quote attributed to the pre-Socratic Greek philosopher, Heraclitus of Ephesus, "No man ever steps in the same river twice, for it's not the same river, and he's not the same man."

Managing change and mitigating the effect of uncertainty is one of a leader's greatest challenges. The most effective leaders not only manage change, they provoke it, and then shape it to the best advantage of the organization. This type of leader looks at uncertainty, not as a problem, but as an opportunity to excel.

Late in my career, I was assigned to head an organization that had been in existence for over fifteen years. During that time the number of tasks and missions assigned to the organization had more than doubled, but there had been no changes in staffing, nor had the organization conducted a review of its procedures and policies. One of the first things I did was to direct a total mission review, to include all of our supporting and associated organizations. I created a mission review team made u of a cross section of employees, making sure to include a few skeptics and diehard bureaucrats in the mix. In an early meeting with the team, as I gave them the concept of what they were being tasked to do I said that the main goal was to build an organization t hat was flexible and enduring. One of the team members looked confused at that statement. When I asked him why he said that my statement sounded like a contradiction. Flexibility means change, while he associated endurance with a fixed state. You are both right and wrong I explained. Flexibility is related to change, but it also refers to the ability to adapt to change, and if an organization is to endure it must above all be able to change itself to meet any and all contingencies. Within a year, we had made major internal procedural changes, and had convinced our higher-level bosses to increase our budget to meet the increased (notice, I don't say increasing, although, the demands *were* actually on an upward trend) demands.

We live in an age of constant change and with each passing year that changed seems to come at a faster pace. When I entered the Foreign Service in 1982 diplomatic messages were laboriously written in multiple copies on a form, which was then given to the communications technicians who had to retype it onto a tape that was fed into a machine for dispatch. Corrections and changes had to be made on each copy and it wasn't at all rare for mistakes to be introduced during the creation of the transmission tapes. By the time I retired in 2012, American diplomats were typing their cables on a computer, sending them electronically to everyone who had to coordinate or provide input, and then electronically to the official who had to approve it. That official then sent it globally with the tap of a key, and thousands of recipients could read it within minutes.

In the early days of the American republic, instructions to our diplomats abroad had to be written (with quill pens) and then dispatched by ship. They had to wait weeks or months for responses to queries, or for instructions to arrive, and because of the uncertainty of weather and mishaps at sea, sometimes they never came. When I became a diplomat in 1982, instructions and responses were sent by telegram (in State Department parlance, cable) or by telephone, greatly shortening the waiting time. Currently, email enables instantaneous transmission of even the most complicated and lengthy messages.

Change and uncertainty are the Castor and Pollux of our modern existence. They come together to constantly challenge leadership. Change causes uncertainty and stress and is usually resisted for that very reason, even when the change is for the better. Great leaders manage change and mitigate uncertainty.

There are a number of ways that change occurs.

1. *Culture shifts.* Leadership guru Warren Bennis, in his book, *Managing People is like Herding Cats*, described culture as the most important avenue of change. Like sand in a wind-swept desert, culture is constantly shifting around us. One only has to look at the way people watch movies today to get a sense of what that means. When I was a kid in the 1950s, if you wanted to watch a movie at home you had to have a projector, a screen and the manual dexterity to thread the unwilling film into the sprockets on the reels. When my own children were kindergarten age in the early 1970s we had video tape. Does anyone remember the culture shift when the beta tape was

replaced by VHS? I was flummoxed. But, not nearly as much as when my entire VHS collection was made obsolete by DVDs. Now, of course, with Netflix™ and Hulu™, and all the other streaming services, all you need is a laptop, or a tablet—some people even watch movies on their smart phones. All that in just a few decades, and its just one aspect of cultural change in the past sixty years.

2. *External events.* Things happening outside an organization, such as social change or government regulations, can have a profound impact on how the organization functions. When I enlisted in the army in 1962, there were few women in the ranks and what few did serve were, for the most part in the medical field or clerical jobs. The movement for equal opportunity and treatment of women and government regulations banning gender discrimination (initially it only applied to noncombat positions, but even that has changed) have changed the face of our uniformed services. A visit to any military hospital will give you a sense of just how significant that change is. As a retire soldier I am entitled to treatment at military hospitals, and I live near the Walter Reed National Military Medical Center in Bethesda, Maryland, so that's where I go for all my medical needs. I am both proud and sad each time I see all the young people, male and female, with missing limbs from the wars in Iraq and Afghanistan. Watching them walk proudly through that hospital on

their prosthetic legs always makes me misty eyed.

3. *By fiat.* On occasion, change is imposed from above. Directions from management dictate what and how a subordinate element is to perform. While circumstances sometimes make this necessary, it is often the cause of much angst and discontent within the organization, especially when it hasn't taken the situation on the ground into consideration. When I was ambassador to Cambodia, for instance, problems in neighboring Vietnam caused thousands of Montagnards to flee to Cambodia. The eastern border areas of that country at that time were under the control of the Vietnamese, and fearing their more powerful neighbor, Cambodian authorities were sending many of the refugees back. Washington directed that I protest this at the highest level of government immediately. There were, however, a few problems with this instruction. It came late on a Saturday night, during a local holiday, so there was no one at home at any of the relevant government offices who could be classified a high government official. The message I was told to deliver didn't take into account the role the Vietnamese were playing in the Cambodian actions. This instruction came at a time when we were working to encourage the Cambodians to do more about human trafficking, and giving them a verbal slap in the face for a situation over which they had no control was going to complicate that to no end. Without going into further detail, just

let me say, that was not my most fun weekend during my three-year tour.

4. *Innovative leadership.* The most effective means of change is that which takes place when innovative and enlightened leaders anticipate the currents of change and get their organizations to move ahead of rather than with or behind the trends. One of the best examples of this was Colin Powell's tenure as the U.S. Secretary of State. Prior to his assumption of the office, State was really a rather impersonal place to work. The focus was on managing American's broader foreign relations. People in Washington and its far-flung outposts were expected to take care of themselves. Leaders were often aloof and impersonal, spending more time dealing with foreign dignitaries than with their own people. This is not to say that they didn't care about people, it's just that in the culture that existed at that time, that's the way it was. Some things were more important than others and taking care of your people, the way I was taught to do it as an army second lieutenant. was way down on the priority list. Powell and his leadership team changed the culture, not by fiat, but by example. He walked around the building, even going directly to junior desk officers to get briefed on a subject rather than summoning their bosses to his office. It was Powell who saw to it that every employee had access to the most modern means of communication, including the Internet. Before he came on board embassies had one

Internet terminal, usually in an isolated room that had to be shared by everyone. I'll never forget the meeting I had with Powell's deputy, Rich Armitage, just before I left Washington to take up my posting as ambassador to Cambodia. After covering the main issues in our relations with Cambodia, Armitage closed the meeting with this injunction: "You might go out there and sign treaties, and make everyone in Washington and Cambodia happy, but if at the end of your tour the people who work for you can't say that they were better for having served under you, you will be a (expletive deleted) failure." That certainly changed the view I'd had of what an ambassador's job was up to that point, but I never forgot it.

Cultural change can be unsettling.

Change, as I have previously indicated, is stressful. Uncontrolled change can damage a smoothly functioning organization; and be fatal to an organization that is already dysfunctional. There are, however, a number of ways a leader can effectively manage change to moderate or minimize its disruptive effect on the health of the organization.

1. *Don't change the labels; make it real.* Even when changes is dictated by fiat, true change cannot be mandated. Mandates can change the signs on the door, titles on the organization charts, and new buzz words to be used in all official correspondence, but they can't change the attitude of the people within the organization. In fact, what mandated change often does is foster quiet resistance that eventually not only undermines the change, but the organization itself. Every organization has a formal structure reflected on paper, and an informal one that actually gets the work done. If the impact of a mandated change on the informal structure has not been considered no really significant change will take place. Never forget; it takes more than fancy titles on an organization chart to make an organization function successfully.

2. *Put the right people in the right jobs.* "You don't hire a cook to build a house." Common sense, right? Even a master chef would be out of his or her depth trying to construct a house. Well, when you're instituting change in an organization, you had better make sure the cook is in the kitchen and the carpenter

is on the saw. I find a tendency in many organizations to assign people primarily on the basis of seniority, with a nod to technical skills. Little or no attention is paid to the person's ability to cope with change. In fact, the selection of people for leadership positions often ignores this trait as well. In over half a century of government employment I have never seen this skill mentioned in a performance evaluation—except for those I have written. New leaders are cautioned to avoid making significant change early in their tenure, to avoid creating implacable resistance to their control of the organization. I agree with this, but not for the reason stated. I must digress to explain what might appear to be a contradiction. In an earlier passage I said that leaders should be agents of change, and here I'm saying that a new leader shouldn't make significant changes early on the job (except in an emergency). Bear with me, and it will become clear. When you first assume a leadership position it's wise to study the situation before making any significant changes, except as noted, in an emergency. Observing gives you the opportunity to assess personnel abilities, to get their jobs done, to accept change, and even more importantly, to be change agents. By taking the time to identify those who are technically competent and comfortable with change, you can build the support teams necessary to make subsequent changes work. You increase the odds of real change taking place. I was once put in charge of an organization that had been in existence for many years but had not changed noticeably from the day it started. Needless to say, it was in trouble, but people inside the organization were trying to solve the problems by working harder doing the same things they'd been doing from the beginning—with the same negative results. During my first six months on the job I made only those changes dictated by regulation, but frequently spoke about the changed I saw on the horizon and the need to adapt to them. I did this in formal meetings and in all my casual encounters with the staff. I instituted a reading program with emphasis on books and articles dealing with change. My first significant change, at the six-month mark, was to establish an informal mission analysis team to address issues of interest to me, and at the same time, to forecast where they thought change would be needed. I made sure the team had at least two people who I had identified as resistant to change, with the rest being younger people who were comfortable with ambiguity and change. The team leader was a young air force lieutenant colonel who impressed me as someone who not only was comfortable with change but welcomed it. Because this was an informal additional duty (they worked after hours and at lunch) and they had no authority to direct anything, it was not seen as a threat to cherished traditional procedures and, like my habit of visiting everyone's office every day, as just another one of the new boss's quirks. After a couple of months, though, an amazing thing began to happen. The group had taken to sharing summaries of their deliberations with co-workers. They questioned old habits and established procedures and brought up questions that soon began to be discussed by employees not connected with the team. The two skeptics in the group became vocal advocates tor 'their' ideas and some of their suggestions mysteriously found their way into formal action proposals coming to my desk from the directorates. Eighteen months after my quirky idea was established a proposal came to me from one of the more conservative directorate chiefs for the creation of a new directorate devoted to strategic initiatives and planning, so that new ideas could be formally instituted in the organization. I could barely restrain a smile of satisfaction when my announcement of the creation of this new directorate not only met with nods of approval from my heretofore 'this is the way we've always done it' directors. Immediately after the announcement, my office was swamped with requests to be assigned to the new directorate. The jewel in the crown, however, came when tie director I had identified as most resistant to change complained that none of his people had been assigned to the new directorate, and he felt that they could offer valuable perspectives to its work. I immediately made a few personnel changes to accommodate this most welcome request.

3. *Involve everyone who is affected by the change.* The stress associated with change can be lessened if everyone in the organization experiencing change is made to feel a part of that change and is given the opportunity to express an opinion on the impact and direction of change. That's a

mouthful, but, in effect, it is saying that if you want people to join you on your journey of change, you have to get them to buy a ticket. Failure to talk through a change with everyone affected by it causes unnecessary conflict within an organization. I learned this lesson the hard way during a particularly windy spring in Chiang Mai, Thailand, when I was the administrative officer of our consulate general there. I call it the 'Eucalyptus Tree Incident'. In 1988, shortly after my arrival, I discovered a serious problem. We were spending thousands of dollars each summer replacing broken window panes in the houses at our residential compound. The high spring winds tore limbs from the Eucalyptus trees lining the compound's streets and smashing them into the windows. This had been happening for more than ten years and while the occupants complained about the broken glass all over the place, no one had made a serious effort to do anything about it. This was my first assignment as an admin officer (I was also the de facto deputy consul general) and I was determined to make a difference. I consulted an outside safety expert and his advice was to trim the trees so their tops were below the level of the top of the houses. That way they would be out of the wind. That seemed a simple solution and it would cost a fraction of what we paid to replace broken windows every year, so I had my general services staff prune the trees the following spring just before the winds started. You'd think the compound residents would've been happy that they didn't have to sweep up broken glass or worry about their kids being cut by glass lying around, but you'd be wrong. They were furious that 'their' trees h ad been mutilated without their consent. While the trees were no 'theirs', as this was a U.S. government property, I saw their point. This was their community, and the ambiance of the waving Eucalyptus trees was part of what they'd come to expect. Had I taken an hour or so to meet with them and explain what I was planning to do, and why, as well as the fact that this species of tree, like grass, grows incredibly fast, and by the end of spring those cut trees had regained all the height we'd lopped off and more, I would've saved myself the several acrimonious meetings afterwards.

4. *Understand the environment in which the change takes place.* The 'War of the Eucalyptus Trees' described above is such an amusing tale—after the fact—yet so instructive, I have often used it in mu discussions with young employees when we talk about implementing change. In addition to showing the importance of involving the people impacted by the change, it underscores the importance of being aware of the environment in which the change occurs. When people live in a foreign country for long periods they try to establish a sense of community. For Americans in a foreign environment, symbols that invoke 'home' are important. Eucalyptus trees aren't quite the same as the elms and maples that line our suburban streets, but in Chiang Mai they were the closest thing. Inside the walls of our

compound people could suspend disbelief and feel as if they were back home in Northern Virginia or suburban Maryland. They didn't like having windows broken or worrying about kids stepping on glass shards, and when I had the trees cut there were no more broken glass. But, all they saw was that some 'fool had our damned trees cut!' With all the best intentions I had failed to take their feelings into account, and a change that was clearly for the better was, at first, bitterly resented and resisted. This happens more than you can imagine in organizations, and the most effective leaders, those who want to be true change agents, are acutely aware of it.

5. *Don't allow the opponents of change to frame the issue.* Measure twice, cut once. This injunction is meant to instill the notion that planning should always take place before action. When making change I think of it as a caution to do all the other things I have listed before embarking on any significant change. In fact, even minor changes, such as trimming trees, should planned carefully. Timing is crucial, as is phased implementation of change. The best way to make real change in an organization, especially one that is resistant to change, is to do it in a way that is initially imperceptible. Get people accustomed to making small changes that don't directly threaten their view of orthodoxy and let them own the changes they make. Don't allow your impatience to get things done cause you to

move too far, too fast. If you back a rabbit into a corner he will fight. Give a bureaucrat the impression that you are about to shake his comfortable routine apart and he will resist. If you don't have a complete picture of your goal in mind and you don't convey that vision to the organization, you can find yourself spending more time fighting the objections than making the change. Energy spent fending off objections to change is wasted. Anticipate objection and obstacles before they appear and develop preemptive countermeasures. Nothing stops an opponent in his tracks quicker than an action addressing a problem before he has even brought it up. Like a good boxer, never telegraph your punches.

6. *Build a support base using those who agree with you.* While the responsibility for making decisions in an organization rests squarely on the shoulders of the leader, making effective and real change required many willing hands—and minds. The decision in June, 1944 to launch the Normandy Invasion was Eisenhower's alone, but the defeat of the Nazis was accomplished through the sacrifices of thousands of soldiers, sailors, airmen, and marines. When planning a change in your organization, remember that you are not working with a blank slate. Those who were there before you arrived have a stake in the organization, knowledge of its history and customs, and in many cases, technical expertise that you lack. Attempts to impose change without enlisting potential allies merely creates unnecessary antagonists.

7. *Have a solid concept of the change you wish to make and what it means to the organization.* If you don't know where you're going you won't know when you get there. Effective change management requires a leader to have the ability to paint a convincing picture of an unknown future state for his or her followers. You must know not only what you wish to change, but how you wish to change it. Making fundamental changes in an organization is best done incrementally. If it is to be enduring it must be gradual, allowing time for people to internalize it. The process of integrating public schools in the U.S. south is an example of incremental change. While the motives of many who supported this method might have been to delay integration, and in many places it was poorly executed, the concept was actually sound. Overcoming more than two centuries of institutionalized segregation could not be achieved overnight. The idea of starting the process in the lower grades and phasing it in year by year, although thought by many to be too little, too late, allowed opponents of integration to gradually become accustomed to what was a fundamental social change. The fact that today there are school age children, of all ages, in my home state of Texas who don't remember whet it was like to attend segregated schools is a testament to the soundness of the method.

Compassion and Empathy

There are leaders, and we all know at least one, who put the job first and consider people as little more than tools to be used as needed. The most effective leaders, though, the truly great leaders, find ways to balance mission and people. In the words of a military adage, 'mission first, people always.'

Now, by compassion and empathy, I'm not talking about pity. As a leader, particularly in government and military organizations, you will be required on occasion to ask (order) people to do difficult, unpleasant, and sometimes dangerous things. Having compassion and empathy doesn't mean that you'll shrink from making these decisions. It does mean, however, that you will do them with full awareness that you're dealing with individuals, and you will ensure that these individuals know that you care for them, and their welfare. Marine Sergeant Michael Strank, one of the men in the Joe Rosenthal photo of the raising of the American flag on Iwo Jima in World War II, is an example of a leader who made the hard calls but did so in a way that let his subordinates know he cared. He shared their hardships, and when leading them into battle, he assured them that his goal was to get everyone back safely, if possible. Michael Strank took an interest in every man in his unit, working to get the best possible performance out of each of them.

During the Vietnam War, officers who 'sent' their men into battle while showing little or no concern for them as individuals were on occasion the victim of friendly fire., or from fragmentation grenades rolled into their tents while they slept. This method of responding to poor leadership was called 'fragging.' Those fortunate enough not to become victims of friendly fire or fragging, often found it difficult to get their men into assault positions, had larger numbers of soldiers going absent without leave (AWOL), or too many men finding long lists of ailments that kept them on 'sick call' to avoid going into combat. I knew others, though, who were in just as many fire fights, took the most dangerous assignments, and always seemed to have a long list of GIs volunteering to go with them. All of these leaders, officers and noncommissioned officers, had gone through the same training and had a similar level of technical skill. The latter, however, had one additional skill, or character trait. Like Sergeant Strank, they genuinely cared for their people. They made sure their men were fed before they themselves ate, and they spent time with their men on and off-duty, getting to know them as individuals. If a soldier under one of these leaders had a personal problem, he knew he could take it to the 'old man,' even if the old man was just a twenty-something year old second lieutenant. When these leaders gave the command to 'charge,' they could concentrate on the enemy and not have to worry about whether or not their men were complying. They never had to watch their backs, because the entire unit was behind them.

Leaders in civilian organizations don't have to worry about being fragged, but employees have their own ways of responding to uncaring supervisors. Absenteeism, missed deadlines, poor quality work and industrial 'accidents' can, in a way, be just as deadly—they can kill a career. You can compel obedience to your directives through fear and coercion up to a point. But, the leader who choses this course can never turn his back. When your subordinates believe that not only know what they're doing, but care about them as unique individuals, they are motived to excel in ways that can't be achieved through force or fear.

The Courage to Take Risks

My grandmother's oldest son, my uncle Buddy, was fond of playing poker, although, he rarely played for more than a nickel or dime per hand. Uncle Buddy was an even-tempered fellow, who rarely showed anger, but whenever he was playing with people who were hesitant to support the hands they held by betting he would get agitated.

Sitting at the table with a player who dithered over his cards, or folded rather than bet, he would roll the ever-present wad of tobacco around in his mouth, spit a stream of the foul, brown juice on the ground or floor, and say, "If you don't bet, you can't win." Of course, you have no idea what the other players are holding and there is a chance that you might lose, but if you don't put your money on the table, the pot will go the last man standing.

Leadership is like poker in that regard. You know the cards in your hand, and if you've been paying attention, you should have some idea of how the other players bet. Sometimes, folding is the best choice, but if you fold on every hand you'll never win. Since you will never have perfect knowledge, though, sometimes you just have to 'put your money on the table.'

My first assignment after being commissioned as a second lieutenant in 1965 was to an artillery battalion in Germany. There were only a limited number of positions in the coveted artillery batteries (the equivalent of an infantry company) for new lieutenants, and by the time I arrived in Hanau, that had all been filled. Rather than send me to another unit, the battalion commander created a special logistics task force and put me in charge. I was also given the additional duty as commander of the aggressor force when the battalion and its sister units went on training exercises. Neither position was on the official Table of Organization and Equipment (TO&E), but I was determined to make the best of it.

My logistics task force was made up of soldiers from other units in the battalion who were either disciplinary problems or were considered subpar performers by their commanders. We were given a rundown old building in the rear of the battalion compound and as long as my guys stayed out of trouble we were pretty much ignored.

For the first two months nothing much happened. We managed to keep the special supplies and parts that are essential to the operations of a mechanized artillery unit flowing in the right amounts to the right places. It wasn't until our first field training exercise, called an FTX, that I was able to instill a sense of pride in my guys, all of whom had been demoralized by the treatment they'd received in their previous units.

For this particular exercise we were assigned to tes the internal security measures of the units in the field. One particular six-gun battery was of special interest. It was commanded by an obnoxious captain, a West Point graduate who viewed enlisted soldiers and officers who received their commissions through ROTC or OCS with equal disdain. He had bragged that if any of my aggressors had the nerve to attack his unit he would have us for breakfast. His battery had nearly a hundred well-trained soldiers and I was in command of ten misfits. No one was betting on our being able to breach his defenses. In fact, given the orthodox thought at the time, you should never attack unless you had a numerical advantage. It was generally believed that we should limit our activity to harassing his outposts. Partly our of a desire to rub his nose in the mud, and partly out of the knowledge that it was the last think anyone would expect, I decided to assault his battery headquarters.

After dark, we made our way slowly past the outposts and concealed our camouflaged bodies in the brush just outside the barbed-wire enclosed area. The eleven of us lay concealed for over four hours, watching as the battery settled down for the night. At 0200 hours, when the sentries were beginning to be drowsy from the boredom of a four-hour shift, we wormed our way through the wire and set dummy charges on equipment and weapons. I was proud of the way my 'misfits' went about their work. The only sounds were the night birds and the snoring of soldiers exhausted from a day of hard training. Little did they know that they were about to get a rude, and loud, wake-up call.

Each of our dummy charges had a smoke grenade attached with a wire attached to the grenade's pin. When all the charges were placed we gathered near the captain's tent and prepared to leave. As a parting gesture I pulled the pin on a tear gas grenade and rolled it into the arrogant captain's tent. Then, I gave the order to haul ass out of the area. One of my men yanked the wire attached to the charges and we dashed toward the main entrance to the enclosure, yelling, 'attack, we're under attack', as we ran. The sentry at the entrance blinked dumbly at us as we ran past, but his attention was quickly drawn to the billowing white smoke that was filling the area, and the sight of his commander stumbling out of his tent in his underwear, rubbing his stinging eyes. By the time the captain was able to recover and get his defense force assembled we were half a kilometer away, rolling on the ground, and laughing so hard we cried.

The captain got a failing grade for security and I was *persona non grata* in the officers' club for weeks afterward. My battalion commander admonished me for using the tear gas grenade, but he had a half-smile on his face as he did it, and my officer fitness report a few months later was filled with glowing phrases describing my initiative—although no mention was ever again made about that specific incident. More importantly, my task force had developed a new sense of self-worth and pride. My guys were no longer the battalion misfits. They began to take more care with their uniforms and general appearance, and to walk around the battalion area with a confident swagger and their heads held high. We were soon taking first place in battalion snap inspections, and when replacements were needed for the battalion honor guard my guys snagged three of the four slots.

Make a decision, even if it's wrong

Decisiveness

"Make a decision even if it's wrong." I can't even remember how many times I heard that phrase when I was in the army. It usually came buried in a string of curses from a drill sergeant trying to motivate a reluctant recruit to take some action—any action—toward completing his assigned mission. The underlying philosophy is that a military unit frozen in place while its commander agonizes over what to do next is vulnerable. A unit on the move, on the other hand, is a harder target for the enemy to hit and has the ability to adjust movement and action to fit changes to the tactical situation.

During my first tour in Vietnam, which began in 1968 shortly after the '68 Tet Offensive, I worked with units that conducted reconnaissance missions deep behind enemy lines. These 12-man Recon Teams (RTs) were lightly armed and not intended to engage in combat with hostile forces. Their mission was to go in, learn what they could, and get out, all hopefully without being spotted by the Viet Cong or the North Vietnamese Army. Unfortunately, the target area was so heavily populated by NVA and VC units, and we were putting so many teams on the ground, it was inevitable that there would be clashes. One particular incident of a compromised recon stands out in my mind because it illustrates how the wrong decision made at the right time can sometimes produce outstanding results.

One of our teams, led by a young staff sergeant, was spotted by a large enemy force shortly after leaving the helicopter landing area, but too late to turn back and be extracted. There were well over 100 well-armed NVA regulars and they soon had the team maneuvered into a small depression in the elephant-grass-covered plain, with its back to a hill. Surrender was not an option. We had good reason to believe that enemy forces had orders to execute our people if captured. Nor was it possible to hold the position for the time it would take for relief forces to arrive from the base camp, though that was the best of the textbook options for situations like they were in. The sergeant reviewed his options, then did something that would have earned him a stern lecture if it had been a training exercise. He lined his team up in a line and yelled, 'Charge'. Twelve camouflaged warriors rose up and dashed headlong at the advancing Vietnamese, yelling and firing their weapons as fast as possible. One can only imagine what must have gone through those NVA soldiers' minds. Whatever it was, it involved anything but fighting these mad men. The entire enemy force broke and ran, fleeing the area as if they were being pursued by devils from the bowels of hell. As soon as he was confident that the enemy was far enough away, and there was an unimpeded route to the extraction point, he called for a cease fire and he and the team made their way to a clearing where they were picked up by helicopter and returned safely to base. The result of this unorthodox maneuver was over 20 NVA killed, with no injuries to the RT.

This was decisive leadership. As Colin Powell said in his autobiography, *My American Journey*, 'Leadership is the art of accomplishing more than the science of management says is possible."

Leadership is the art of motivating people to achieve goals; it is making decisions. In the performance evaluation system for Foreign Service Officers, the State Department rates employees in a number of areas. As you might imagine, many of these performance traits have to do with diplomacy, from cultural sensitivity and foreign language skill. A large part of a diplomat's performance evaluation, however, revolves around leadership, and decision making is a key component of that leadership. The following description of effective decision making is taken from the instructions for rated and rating officials:

"Makes measured, effective, and timely decisions after considering all *relevant* (emphasis mine) factors and options, even when data are limited or confliction or will produce unpleasant consequences; implements decisions and evaluates their impact and implications, making adjustments as needed."

Or, as my old drill sergeant would say, 'make a decision, even if it's wrong."

Inquisitiveness

In the previous section I stressed that a leader has to make decisions with less than perfect knowledge of a situation. This does not mean that he or she shouldn't be constantly seeking more information. A truly effective leader, of for that matter, any effective person, should be a sponge for information, soaking up every morsel available, and, like the mouse sniffing for cheese, constantly looking for more. Learning should be a life-long process with new skills added and old skills upgraded on a continuing basis. You can never *really* know too much.

When I left East Texas in 1962 and joined the army I only had a high school diploma from a segregated school which was probably worth almost the cost of the paper it was printed on. I'm not gratuitously insulting Booker T. Washington High School, just pointing out that minority schools in the era when I was a student were at the end of the line for books and equipment—we got the used stuff that the white school discarded when they bought new stuff. The first time I had a brand-new text book was when I enrolled in college courses in the army. So, a graduate from a minority school in Texas who didn't go on to one of the historical black colleges like Texas Southern, Prairie View, or Wiley, was considered qualified for work as a common laborer for less than minimum wage. I had a $500 scholarship to Prairie View, a stipend awarded to each valedictorian of the black high schools around the state, but coming from a poor rural family, had no clue where the other funds I would need would come from. So, college was out for the immediate future, and I wasn't about to take a menial job. In addition, from reading the *National Geographic* magazines that my step-father's older sister kept stacked in her living room I had developed an insatiable desire to see the world. So, I enlisted in the army.

After training and my first tour of duty as a radio operator (who seldom operated a radio) in Germany, I returned to the U.S., attended OCS, and was commissioned as a second lieutenant. I was sensitive to the fact that I only had a high school diploma, and felt that an officer, even one who wasn't at the time planning to make the army a career, should be well educated, so I began taking night classes at colleges near the posts where I was stationed, or enrolling in the overseas courses that a lot of colleges like University of Maryland and University of Southern California have established for military personnel serving overseas. I also read everything I could get my hands on and began collecting books (I now have approximately 9,000 volumes on a variety of subjects, both fiction and nonfiction).

By 1971, I'd earned more than enough academic hours for my bachelor's degree but didn't have the required number of credits earned in residence at any of the more than ten schools I'd studied at over the previous nine years. Fortunately, the army had a program that allowed soldiers who had earned enough credits to be within a semester of graduation to enroll full time in college while continuing to collect army pay. I don't recall the official name of the program, but it was popularly called the Bootstrap Program for obvious reasons. Benedictine College, a small Catholic college in Atchison, Kansas, accepted me as a senior working for a B.S. in business administration. Because of the credits I'd accrued over the years I was only required to take 18 hours of business courses, to satisfy the department's requirements, leaving me six hours to play with, so I took courses in psychology to fulfill my 24-hour residency requirement. In addition, I joined the drama club, where I helped stage productions and designed sets and brochures, and played on the football team, where I spent most of the season on the bench. But, since I was the only active duty soldier on the team, and was older than the head coach, I was something of a celebrity.

Prior to enrolling in Benedictine College, I had spent a year at the Defense Intelligence College in Washington, DC, studying strategic intelligence, having transferred to the military intelligence branch from artillery the year before.

After graduation in 1972, I was sent back to Vietnam for my second tour, assigned to the 525th Military Intelligence Group. By now, I was a senior captain, one of the more senior captains in the group, but every other officer in the outfit had many more years of intelligence experience than I did. Despite my lack of experience, the group commander put me in charge of the section responsible for all intelligence collection for the Military Assistance Command (MACV), supervising ten intelligence officers who had been working in intelligence their entire careers. His reasoning when I expressed doubt about my qualifications to handle such a sensitive assignment was that he needed someone in charge who had more than just technical expertise. Ensuring the efficient and effective employment of intelligence resources to support military operations throughout Vietnam required a broad understanding of the environment and the needs of operational commanders. My previous experience managing strategic reconnaissance operations during my first tour, and my education and training in business, he believed, would make up for my lack of technical intelligence experience. In addition, he told me, the fact that I had taken courses in a broad range of disciplines rather than concentrating in one field led him to believe I would bring creativity to the job and not be a slave to the 'book' solution. The officers in my section, like me, all had to six to ten years of service, but, unlike the others who had served as intelligence officers for their entire careers, by 1972 I had been a supply officer in an artillery unit, a strategic reconnaissance planner, and had served for six months as a counterintelligence plans officer responsible for developing domestic counterintelligence policy, and an infantry training company officer. In addition, I had taught myself to speak German, spent ten months in Washington, DC learning Vietnamese, and taken courses in psychological operations, unconventional warfare, and civil affairs. I was master of no skill, but the 'Jack of all trades' he sought for that particular job.

Self Confidence

When you make a decision, you have to believe that you have done the right thing. This is more than just the courage to take risks; it is an internalized belief in yourself and your abilities. If you project belief in yourself, others will believe in you. Being self-confident does not mean that you will never make a mistake, but it means that you have a strong enough sense of self to identify, admit, and learn from your mistakes.

Some people are probably born with self-confidence. Most infants that I've seen are fearless until they get hurt, or life and the educational system puts fear into them. My grandson, Tommy, though, seems to be one of those rare people who just exude self-confidence. At three years of age, he delights in climbing to the top rung of the jungle gym his parents bought him and his two older sisters and hanging upside down. He's fallen from high places in the house and busted his lip a few times, but he keeps going back and trying again until he gets it right. His sister, Catie, the number two child, is also a very self-confident person, but with a different personality. She examines a new challenge from all sides until she has decided on the best way to attack it, and then she's all in. She was the only one of my grandchildren who never crawled. She lay on her stomach or back and watched her older sister, Samantha, who is two years older, walk, and when she got the hang of it, she pushed herself upright and walked across the room.

People like Tommy and Catie are rare. Most of us learn to fear things at an early age, and the self-confidence, which is born out of ignorance of the perils, just evaporates.

At any rate, my theory of those naturally self-confident people is that, like my grandchildren, they were born with it, and through the luck of the draw, or some superior gene, refused to give it up. For the rest of us self-confidence is like any other skill. If we want to get it back, we have to practice it. Like learning the piano or how to ride a bicycle, if you practice often enough and long enough, you can get the hang of it. You might not become a virtuoso, but you'll do okay. As you succeed, you become more confident. When you fail, and believe me, you will fail, learn from your mistake, pick yourself up, and try again. As my grandmother said to me what seems like a million times,

> **"It doesn't matter how many times you fall down, only how many times you get back up."**

I took up the game of golf at the ripe young age of 50, because so many of my diplomatic colleagues played, and this gave me more opportunities to network with them. The 'veteran' golfers among the Ho Chi Minh City foreign consular corps were the British, Dutch, and the Singaporean, and they welcomed me and were very friendly, offering advice and letting me tag along as I learned the basics of the game. One sage bit of advice they gave; 'Don't let it get you down. The golden standard of golf for a beginner is to break 100. But, fewer than ten percent of the people who take this game up ever make it.' They also cautioned me that, staring the game so late in life it was unlikely that I would *ever* shoot a game under a hundred.

I, on the other hand, had a different opinion about my ability. I'd been a gawky, unathletic teenager with two left feet who managed with great effort to make the high school varsity basketball team—and, even in a school as small as ours, it wasn't easy—I was captain of my high school track team, and I played college football at 26. When I was in the army, I coached little league baseball and played on my battalion basketball team. I was always number one or two in the mile run when my unit did the physical training test. I was realistic enough to know that I would never be a scratch golfer (someone who shoots the course par, normally 72, and has a zero handicap), but with practice, hitting the ball less than a hundred times in eighteen holes was a goal that I should be able to reach. I bought an old set of clubs from the South Korean consul general, read as much about the game as I could, and went to the local driving range several times a week. After a few weeks, I talked my aforementioned friends, the British, Dutch, and Singaporean consul general, into letting me and my clubs tag along with them. I watched what they did and adapted it to my own physique. A digression here. I have extraordinarily long arms. My reach is about an inch longer than the average person my height. So, if someone with shorter arms tries to tell me how to swing a club or bat, it won't work. Those longer arms, by the way, contribute to greater club head speed—I won't explain that, because the physics is complicated, just trust me, they do. Anyway, I kept plugging away, playing whenever I had free time. Eleven months after I played my first complete eighteen holes, I shot 97, and in a tournament no less. Nine months after that, thanks to birdies on the last three holes I shot 89, and since then, I've enjoyed the game, shooting in the mid-nineties on average, with the occasional game in the high eighties. Some people would call my approach to golf cocky, but I never bragged about it—well, I did crow a bit when I shot that 97—I just quietly went about doing what I thought I could do and ignored the naysayers. That is just self-confidence.

Self-confident leadership is the same. You have to have faith that you can use the skills you have, improve the weak ones, and get the job done. When I was consul general in Ho Chi Minh City I was responsible for mentoring and professional development of the junior FSOs assigned to the consulate general. My words to them on self-confident leadership were simple. I contrasted leadership with management. What I told them was this: a good manager is someone who can keep several balls in the air at the same time. A good leader is someone who knows which balls can be dropped without jeopardizing the mission, and a great leader is someone who has enough self-confidence to go ahead and drop them.

Motivation

Motivation, or drive, is a trait that all successful leaders have. Motivation alone, however, is no guarantee of success. When motivation leads an individual to seek power as an end in itself it can lead to colossal failure. Adolph Hitler is a prime example of a leader with a great drive who sought power and displayed a willingness to do anything to gain and hold on to it. His motivation nearly destroyed Germany and embroiled the world in a conflagration, whose effects are still apparent in many areas to the present day.

You must have the desire to lead if you want to be successful. But, that desire must be for the right reason. As my grandmother would say:

> **"The right thing done passably well is better than the wrong thing done perfectly."**

Leadership is not just about doing things right, but doing the right things, and doing them for the right reasons.

Intelligence

Earlier in the book I talked about the need to make learning a life-long activity. Learning, I believe, leads not only to knowledge but increases intelligence. A successful leader has to be able to interpret and integrate large and diverse amounts of information. This required intelligence or cognitive ability, but even the experts disagree on just how much. Like motivation, intelligence alone does not guarantee success. No one can argue that lack of cognitive skills or intelligence will lead to poor results, but is it possible to be too smart? Here we go with that 'angels on the head of a pin' argument again. I must confess that I don't have an answer, other than to repeat the phrase attributed to Abraham Lincoln when he was asked how long a man's legs should be, and he answered, 'long enough to reach the ground." My own experience and observations have led me to conclude that for a successful leader, having a high IQ is less important than the ability to continually learn and adapt to ever changing circumstances. You might never change you measured IQ, but you'll develop knowledge, skills, and abilities that will make people look at you in a positive light.

If You're Not a Born Leader—Reinvent Yourself

According to the *great person* theory of leadership, great leaders possess traits that set them apart from the average person. Are people really 'born' to lead, or can leadership be learned? There have been many great people throughout history, from Alexander the Great to Martin Luther King, Jr., who had traits that clearly raised them above the herd, so it's clear that traits do matter, and that some people seem to have just been born with the 'right stuff.' Taken along with other factors these traits contribute to successful leadership. What is not clear is whether or not the ability to effectively match these traits with the other factors effectively is an innate skill or learned behavior. In other words, did these great men make the situation, or did the situation make them?

Despite the military's many schools to 'train' leaders, and despite (or perhaps because of) my own extensive exposure to that training, I have come to the conclusion that leadership can't be *taught*, but that it can be *learned*. Each leadership situation, each organization, each individual is unique and require a different combination of applications of personal abilities and external factors in order to be effective. While there are some solid leadership principles, there is no recipe, or 'book solution' that you can be taught that will apply to all situations. You can, however, learn to assess a situation and use your ability to shape and direct it. If you're weak in certain areas, you can, either with the help of teachers or through self-study, improve them.

How do you learn to lead? Back in East Texas the old folks used to say, you learn to swim by getting in the water. Leading is like swimming—you learn to do it by doing it. The State Department has diplomats in residence at several colleges and universities around the country who recruit people for the department's Foreign and Civil Services. They also conduct—or did when I was one—training to prepare students to take the Foreign Service written exam and oral assessment.

In the past, these were experienced, senior people who also lectured and taught international relations at the schools and in the communities where they were assigned. Recently, State began assigning more junior officers to these jobs to focus solely on recruiting, which is a shame. While they can still be a voice for American diplomacy, they lack the gravitas to be effective in all situation and passing along knowledge that makes young people better leaders is, in my opinion, one of the most important functions the diplomats in residence performed.

When I was diplomat in residence at the University of Houston during the 2005-2006 school year I was often asked how best to prepare for the written exam, a half-day test that is the first step on the road to becoming an FSO. My response was that the only way to be successful on the exam was to take it. Only about one in four pass it on the first try, but if a person truly has the desire, a second, third, and sometimes a fourth effort is often successful. Learning to lead is the same. If you really want to learn to be a successful leader, you can only achieve that goal by leading. Like swimming, you start in the shallow water, gradually moving into the deeper water when your confidence and ability develops. Unless you're one of those gifted people who just have it all together and you get everything right the first time, you'll make mistakes. Learn from your mistakes and move on. As you learn, just remember this—it's not how many times you fall down that's important, it's how many times you get back up again.

Charles Ray

Bibliography

There is a rich selection of literature on leadership, and reading should be a key part of your life-long learning program. While reading should focus on those areas most relevant to your specific situation, I also recommend casting a wide net. Leadership principles can be found throughout literature, even in fiction. In this selected bibliography I have listed those books that I have found particularly useful in my career leading military and civilian government organizations, and, since my retirement in 2012, in academic and commercial pursuits.

Bennis, Warren, *Managing People is Like Herding Cats,* Executive Excellence Publishing, Provo, Utah. 1999.

-----, *Old Dogs, New Tricks,* Executive Excellence Publishing, Provo, Utah. 1999

Brown, Anthony Cave, *The Last Hero, Wild Bill Donovan,* Times Books, New York. 1982.

von Clausewitz, Karl, *On War,* Princeton University Press, Princeton, NJ. 1976.

Freedman, David H., *Corps Business: The 30 Management Principles of the U.S. Marines*, HarperBusiness, New York. 2000.

Greenberg, Jerald, *Managing Behavior in Organizations*, Prentice Hall, Upper Saddle river, NJ. 1996.

Hart, J.H. Liddell, *Strategy* (second revised edition), Penguin Books, New York. 1991.

Johnson, Spencer, M.D., *Who Moved My Cheese?*, G.P. Putnam Books, New York. 1998.

Maurer, Rick, *Why Don't You Want What I Want?*, Bard Press, Austin, TX. 2002.

Mayer, Martin, *The Diplomats*, Doubleday and Company, New York. 1983.

McMaster, H.R., *Dereliction of Duty, Lyndon Johnson, Robert McNamara, The Joint Chiefs od Staff, and the Lies That Led to Vietnam*, HarperCollins Publishers, New York. 1997.

Morin, Ann Miller, *Her Excellency: An Oral History of American Women Ambassadors*, Twayne Publishers, New York. 1995.

Moskin, Robert, *Mr. Truman's War*, Random House, New York. 1996.

Phillips, Donald T., *Lincoln on Leadership: Executive Strategies for Tough Times*, Warner Books, New York. 1992.

----, *Martin Luther King, Jr. on Leadership: Inspiration & Wisdom for Challenging Times*, Warner Books, New

York. 1999.

Powell, Colin, with Joseph E. Persico, *My American Journey*, Random House, New York. 1995.

Shaevitz, Marjorie Hansen, *The Confident Woman*, Harmony Books, New York. 1999.

Tzu, Sun, *The Art of War* (translated by Samuel B. Griffith), Oxford University Press, London. 1963.

Wachs, William, *The Successful Manager's Guide*, Parker Publishing Company, West Nyack, NY. 1967.

Wofford, Jerry C., with Edwin A. Gertoff and Robert C. Cummins, *Organizational Communication: The Keystone to Managerial Effectiveness*, McGraw Hill, New York. 1977.

Smith, Perry M., *Taking Charge: A Practical Guide for Leaders,* National Defense University Press, Washington, DC, 1986.

The discerning reader can also find some effective leadership principles in works of fiction, but because taste in fiction is a highly personal thing, I have not listed any books here. I'm a voracious reader but am a special fan of science fiction. I am particularly fond of Gene Roddenberry's *Star Trek* series and find it fascinating to study the leadership characteristics of the main characters, the starship captains who 'go boldly where no one has gone before.'

James Tiberius Kirk, the first captain of *Enterprise* (at least, on the original TV series) is an example of a charismatic, hands-on leader who shows how effectiveness can be achieved by breaking the rules.

Jean Luc Picard of *The Next Generation* is a solid by-the-book leader who knows how to get the best out of his crew.

Jane Greenway, captain of *Voyager*, shows how to learn from mistakes and extricate yourself from impossible situations.

Benjamin Sisko, commander of *Deep Space Nine*, is the ultimate cat herder. Successfully forging an extremely diverse group of beings into a winning team.
Jonathan Archer is the first earthbound human to travel into space using warp technology in the very first ship named *Enterprise*. In this prequel to the *Star Trek* series, Archer demonstrates how to deal with uncertainty.

A Final Note

In the original edition of this book, I began this section by saying that we live in stressful times. After the 2016 presidential elections, I rethought that view, and have decided that times in 2006 – 2008 were really not so bad by comparison. With the erratic behavior of some of our senior leadership, hyper-partisanship creating turmoil throughout the country, the war in Afghanistan and other parts of the Middle East now having lasted longer than the Vietnam War, and lack of serious reaction to climate change threatening all life on the planet, we live in perhaps the most stressful times ever.

I believe that it is our sacred obligation as leaders to achieve our goals without adding unnecessarily to that stress, either on ourselves or on others. Since this book was published, I have been doing a lot of thinking about leadership, and in the course of my research have come up with a new tag line that I think describes the kind of leadership we need. In researching my book, *Ethical Dilemmas and the Practice of Diplomacy*, it occurred to me that finding effective strategies to deal with the many ethical gray areas that diplomats encounter on a routine basis, also applies to those who must lead in these uncertain, ethically-ambiguous times.

I hope that readers will find some useful nuggets of wisdom in this modest book. If you find it helpful, I am not the one you need to think. Some of the kudos go to Michael Keller, who first suggested I write it, but the lion's share of the credit has to go to my grandmother, Sally Young, who, while putting me through Aunt Sally's School of Leadership and Management in the 1950s, instilled in me the will to overcome any obstacle, meet any challenge, and most of all, leave the world a better place.

If you find the book useful, I again ask that you take a few minutes and leave a review, even a word or two, on Amazon, Goodreads, or whichever site you bought it from.

Books by this author:

Al Pennyback mysteries
Color Me Dead
Memorial to the Dead
Deadline
Dead, White, and Blue
A Good Day to Die
The Day the Music Died
Die, Sinner
Deadly Intentions
Death by Design
Till Death Do Us Part
Deadly Dose
Dead Man's Cove
Dead Men Don't Answer
Deadly Paradise
Kiss of Death
Death in White Satin
Death and Taxis
Deadbeat
A Deadly Wind Blows
Death Wish
Deadly Vendetta
A Time to Kill, A Time to Die
Dead Ringer
Death of Innocence
Dead Reckoning
Murder on the Menu
Over My Dead Body
Bad Girls Don't Die
A Deal to Die For

Ed Lazenby mysteries

Butterfly Effect
Coriolis Effect
The Cat in the Hatbox
Negative Side Effects
Murder is as Easy as ABC

Buffalo Soldier series
Buffalo Soldier: Trial by Fire
Buffalo Soldier: Homecoming
Buffalo Soldier: Incident at Cactus Junction
Buffalo Soldier: Peacekeepers
Buffalo Soldier: Renegade
Buffalo Soldier: Escort Duty
Buffalo Soldier: Battle at Dead Man's Gulch
Buffalo Soldier: Yosemite
Buffalo Soldier: Comanchero
Buffalo Soldier: Range War
Buffalo Soldier: Mob Justice
Buffalo Soldier: Chasing Ghosts
Buffalo Soldier: The Piano
Buffalo Soldier: Family Feud
Buffalo Soldier: The Lost Expedition

Other fiction
Angel on His Shoulder
She's No Angel
Child of the Flame
Pip's Revenge
Wallace in Underland
Further Adventures of Wallace in Underland
Dead Letter and Other Tales
The White Dragons
The Dragon's Lair
Dragon Slayer
The Last Gunfighters
The Culling
Frontier Justice: Bass Reeves, Deputy U.S. Marshal

Angel on His Shoulder-Revised Edition
Battle at the Galactic Junkyard
Mountain Man
Devil's Lake
Vixen
Wagons West: Daniel's Journey
Wagons West: Trinity
Awakening
Fatal Encounters: The Adventures of Bass Reeves, Deputy U.S. Marshal
Dead Letters and Other Tales: Revised edition

Nonfiction
Things I Learned from My Grandmother About Leadership and Life
Taking Charge: Effective Leadership for the Twenty-first Century
Grab the Brass ring
African Places: A Photographic Journey Through Zimbabwe and southern Africa
A Portrait of Africa
There's Always a Plan B
In the Line of Fire: American Diplomats in the Trenches
Advice for the Insecure Writer
Looking at Life Through My Lens
Ethical Dilemmas and the Practice of Diplomacy
Making America Grate Again
DC Street Art
Things I Learned from My Grandmother about Leadership and Life (2d edition)

Children's books
The Yak and the Yeti
Samantha and the Bully

Charles Ray

Molly Learns to Share
Where is Teddy?
Catie and Mister Hop-Hop
Tommy Learns to Count
Catie Goes to School

About the Author

Charles Ray has been writing fiction since his teens. He won a Sunday school magazine writing contest when he was thirteen and having his byline on a short story published in a national publication forever hooked him on writing. During his time in the army (1962-1982) he often moonlighted as a newspaper or magazine journalist and was the editorial cartoonist for the Spring Lake (NC) News, a weekly newspaper, during the 1970s. In addition to his writing, he was an artist/cartoonist and photographer for a number of publications, including Ebony, Eagle and Swan, and Essence, and had a monthly cartoon feature and did several covers for Buffalo, a now-defunct magazine that was dedicated to showcasing the contributions of African-Americans to the country's military history.

After retiring from the army, he joined the U.S. Foreign Service, and served as a diplomat in posts in Asia and Africa until his retirement in 2012. He has worked and traveled throughout the world (Antarctica is the only continent he hasn't visited), and now, as a full-time writer, continues to globetrot looking for interesting things to write about, draw, or take pictures of.

A native of Texas, he now calls Maryland home. For more on his writing and other projects, check one of the following Web sites:

http://charlesaray.blogspot.com
http://charlieray45.wordpress.com
http://www.twitter.com/charlieray45
http://www.facebook.com/charlieray45
http://www.flickr.com/photos/charlesray45/

http://www.viewbug.com/member/charlesray

You can also order some of my books through my author's website: http://charlesray-author.com/

Authors write to be read, and that can only happen when readers are made aware of the books available. Reviews are one way this happens. If you liked this book, please leave a review, even if only a few words, on Amazon or Goodreads.

www.ingramcontent.com/pod-product-compliance
Lightning Source LLC
Chambersburg PA
CBHW071100240526
45471CB00016B/2206